DK EYEWITNESS

T0063744

TOP 10
HONOLULU
AND O'AHU

Top 10 Honolulu and Oʻahu Highlights

The Top 10 of Everything

CONTENTS

Honolulu and Oʻahu Area by Area

Streetsmart

Within each Top 10 list in this book, no hierarchy of quality or popularity is implied. All 10 are, in the editor's opinion, of roughly equal merit.
   Throughout this book, floors are referred to in accordance with American usage; i.e., the "first floor" is at ground level.

Title page, front cover and spine Sunrise over Mokulua Islands, viewed from Lanakai Beach, Oʻahu
Back cover, clockwise from top left Tiki masks at Aloha Stadium Swap Meet, Byodo-in Temple, a tropical beach in Kāhala, Waikīkī Beach, surfing in Oʻahu

The rapid rate at which the world is changing is constantly keeping the DK Eyewitness team on our toes. While we've worked hard to ensure that this edition of Honolulu and Oʻahu is accurate and up-to-date, we know that opening hours alter, standards shift, prices fluctuate, places close and new ones pop up in their stead. So, if you notice we've got something wrong or left something out, we want to hear about it. Please get in touch at **travelguides@dk.com**

Welcome to
Honolulu and Oʻahu

Brilliant reef fish patrol turquoise coves. Sandy beaches are shaded by palm trees swaying in the breeze. Inland, waterfalls cascade down from forested volcanic mountain ridges. This is Oʻahu, Hawaii's third-largest island and home to diverse and lively Honolulu. With DK Eyewitness Top 10 Honolulu and Oʻahu, it's yours to explore.

Settled more than 1,500 years ago by Polynesians, Oʻahu attracted subsequent waves of immigrants from around the world. Most people live in the vicinity of **Honolulu**, a city that reflects its multicultural history through its range of cultural sites and varied cuisine.

Honolulu's star attraction is the iconic **Waikīkī Beach**, but there's a host of things to see in this lively city. Learn about Oʻahu's history and culture by visiting the **ʻIolani Palace**, the **Bishop Museum**, the **Honolulu Museum of Art**, the **Polynesian Cultural Center**, and World War II battleground **Pearl Harbor**. Farther afield, the crater of the dormant **Diamond Head** volcano offers spectacular views of the island, while the wild **North Shore** is the perfect place for keen surfers. Those less comfortable on a board can snorkel in **Hanauma Bay** and spot green sea turtles and manta rays, then see more marine animals at the **Waikīkī Aquarium**. The **Byodo-in Temple**, where wild peacocks wander and guests meditate by the koi-filled ponds, is another highlight on Oʻahu.

Whether you're visiting for a weekend or a week, our Top 10 guide brings together the best of everything the island has to offer. The guide has useful tips throughout, from seeking out what's free to finding the best beaches, plus eight easy-to-follow itineraries designed to tie together a clutch of sights in a short space of time. Add inspiring photography and detailed maps, and you've got the essential pocket-sized travel companion. **Enjoy the book, and enjoy Honolulu and Oʻahu**.

Clockwise from top: Koʻolau Mountain Range, King Kamehameha Statue, Diamond Head Crater, Waikiki Beach, fresh plumeria blossoms, Byodo-in Temple, surfing at Hanauma Bay

Exploring Honolulu and Oʻahu

The island of Oʻahu is full of impressive sights to see and memorable activities to partake in. The following two-day and seven-day itineraries combine some of the best of these and are arranged to make the most of your time on the island.

Key
— Two-day itinerary
— Seven-day itinerary

Bishop Museum
Liliha Bakery
IWILEI
Chinatown
Hawaii State Art Museum
Capitol District
ʻIolani Palace
Honolulu Museum of Art
ALA MOANA

0 km 1
0 miles 1

Waikīkī Beach attracts both visitors and locals with its fine white sand.

Two Days in Honolulu and Oʻahu

Day ❶
MORNING
Hike the **Manoa Falls Trail** *(see p42)*. Afterwards stroll along **Waikīkī Beach** *(see p78)*.

AFERNOON
Take the trolley to the **Honolulu Museum of Art** *(see pp24–5)*, then walk to ʻIolani Palace *(see pp18–19)* and take a self-guided tour. Walking northwest, head into the **Capitol District** *(see pp16–17)* and **Chinatown** *(see pp22–3)*, and sample some street food from the market stalls.

Day ❷
MORNING
Start from Honolulu at 6am, bring a picnic, and drive to **Hanauma Bay** at **South Shore** *(see pp28–9)* for snorkeling without the crowds.

AFTERNOON
Eat a plate lunch at the **Rainbow Drive-In** *(see p59)* and hike the **Diamond Head Trail** *(see p46)*. For dinner get take-out from **Me Bar-B-Q** *(see p81)* in Waikīkī and watch surfers take to the waves at **Kūhiō Beach Park** *(see p26)*.

Seven Days in Honolulu and Oʻahu

Day ❶
Take the trolley to the **Honolulu Museum of Art** *(see pp24–5)* and have lunch at the café. After a self-guided tour of ʻIolani Palace *(see pp18–19)*, go to **Chinatown** and check out the many art galleries *(see pp22–3)*. Dine at **The Pig and the Lady** *(see p75)*.

Day ❷
Go to **Hanauma Bay** at **South Shore** *(see pp28–9)* for snorkeling at 7am when the air is cool and the crowds are still sleeping. Have brunch at **Mud Hen Water** *(see p75)*, then hike the

Diamond Head Trail, a scenic vantage point

Hawaii State Art Museum *(see p17)*. Later, sip poolside cocktails at **Mahina and Sun's** *(see p81)*. Stay to dine on modern local cuisine.

Day ❺
Drive up Pali Hwy, stopping at **Nu'uanu Pali Lookout** *(see p69)*, and head to the **Kāne'ohe District** *(see pp30–31)* to visit the **Byodo-in Temple** *(see p31)* at the Valley of the Temples Memorial Park. Go for a swim at **Lanikai Beach** *(see p49)*, hailed as one of the world's best beaches, followed by a fabulous dinner at **Haleiwa Joe's** *(see p101)* in Kāne'ohe.

Day ❻
Drive to the **North Shore** *(see pp82–7)* and watch surfers take on the big waves. Have lunch at **Giovanni's Shrimp Truck** *(see p87)*. Continue on to the **Polynesian Cultural Center** *(see pp32–3)* and explore the Pacific Island exhibits. In the evening, indulge in some fine seafood dining at **Alaia** *(see p101)* at **Turtle Bay Resort**.

Day ❼
Hike the **Manoa Falls Trail** *(see p42)*, then refuel with a hearty plate lunch at the **Rainbow Drive-In** *(see p59)*. Shop in the Royal Hawaiian Center and other stores along **Kalākaua Avenue** *(see pp26–7)*, then enjoy a delicious dinner at **Sansei Seafood Restaurant & Sushi Bar** *(see p81)* in Waikīkī.

Diamond Head Trail *(see p46)*. Enjoy a sunset cocktail at **Duke's Waikīkī** *(see p80)*, a beloved watering hole.

Day ❸
Visit **Pearl Harbor** *(see pp12–13)*. Go early and plan to spend a full morning exploring the site. Drive to the **Ko Olina Beach Park** lagoons *(see p48)* for swimming. Dine at **Monkeypod Kitchen** *(see p95)*.

Day ❹
Visit the world's largest collection of fine Hawaiian art in the Picture Gallery at **Bishop Museum** *(see pp14–15)*, then stop at **Liliha Bakery** *(see p59)* for a snack. Take the trolley to the **Capitol District** *(see pp16–17)* and visit the

The Manoa Falls Trail snakes through lush vegetation to reach a waterfall.

Top 10 Honolulu and Oʻahu Highlights

Statue of King Kamehameha in front of ʻIolani Palace, Honolulu

Honolulu and Oʻahu Highlights

Oʻahu's main hub is the city of Honolulu. Most visitors make Waikīkī, Honolulu's most famous neighborhood, their base, venturing out from here on day trips to see the city's cultural attractions, Pearl Harbor, and other parts of the island. South Shore and Kāneʻohe District are in striking distance of Honolulu, and the Polynesian Cultural Center is an easy day trip from the city, while surfers head for the North Shore.

0 km 2
0 miles 2

1 Pearl Harbor

This World War II site memorializes the lives lost to the bombings that took place here in 1941 and offers a range of tours *(see pp12–13)*.

3 Capitol District

The State Capitol and the former home of Queen Liliʻuokalani are just some of the attractions of this historic district in Honolulu. *(see pp16–17)*.

2 Bishop Museum

This state museum offers a fascinating insight into Hawaiian culture. Its Science Garden represents the unique Hawaiian land divisions called *ahupuaʻa (see pp14–15)*.

4 ʻIolani Palace

Built for King Kalākaua and Queen Kapiʻolani in the 1800s, the palace was later the seat of government. It is open to the public *(see pp18–19)*.

5 Chinatown

This historic 15-block district is home to gift shops, food purveyors, restaurants, *lei* stands, farmers' markets, and art galleries *(see pp22–3)*.

Honolulu Museum of Art ⑥

Arts of the Islamic and Asian worlds are well represented in this museum, as well as a further 15,000 works by American and European artists. Polynesian works are displayed too *(see pp24–5)*.

⑦ Kalākaua Avenue

Waikīkī's main thoroughfare runs along the ocean up to the crater of Diamond Head. Halfway along the avenue are the "Pink Lady" and the "White Lady" – two landmark hotels *(see pp26–7)*.

⑧ South Shore

The South Shore of Oʻahu has among its many attractions several popular beaches, walking trails over Koko Head, and an underwater park at Hanauma Bay *(see pp28–9)*.

⑨ Kāneʻohe District

A stunning region northeast of Honolulu, Kāneʻohe has a scenic coastline, lush gardens, and state parks *(see pp30–31)*.

⑩ Polynesian Cultural Center

On the north shore of Oʻahu, this center explores the culture, cuisines, and traditions of Hawaiʻi, Tahiti, Tonga, and other Pacific islands *(see pp32–3)*.

TOP 10 ⭐ Pearl Harbor

Set in a bay where Hawaiians once harvested clams and oysters (hence the "pearl" connection), the infamous World War II site is still a key military base. The harbor's relics and memorials, which incorporate the resting place of the battleship *Arizona* and final berth of the historic *USS Missouri*, are visited by nearly 2 million people each year. A museum of military aviation is also nearby.

1 USS Arizona Memorial

Floating above the ship that became a tomb, this stark-white, rectangular structure contains a memorial wall **(left)** where the names of those who lost their lives are inscribed.

2 Battleship Missouri Memorial

Admission to the *USS Missouri* **(right)** offers a standard guided tour or self-guided audio-tour, while the Heart of the Missouri Tour gives a close-up view of the inner workings of the massive battleship.

3 Deck of Surrender

A bronze floor plaque **(below)** in the deck on the *USS Missouri* marks the spot where a mess table was set up on September 2, 1945 for Japanese ministers to sign the Instrument of Surrender agreement in Tokyo Bay.

5 Pearl Harbor Aviation Museum

Found in the middle of Pearl Harbor, Ford Island is home to this museum where most exhibits are housed inside World War II-era hangars. Over 50 aircraft are on display and there's also a flight simulator ride.

4 Ford Island Trail

This 4-mile (6.4-km) paved trail follows the perimeter of Ford Island, which was ground zero for the 1941 attack. Dotted along the way are interpretive signs which detail information on the island's history.

NEED TO KNOW

MAP D5

USS Arizona Memorial: open 7am–5pm daily; www.recreation.gov

Battleship Missouri Memorial: open 8am–4pm daily; $34.99 adults, $17.49 children; www.ussmissouri.org

Ford Island Trail: access via free shuttle bus from the Pearl Harbor Visitor Center every 15 min; open 8am–4pm daily

Pearl Harbor Aviation Museum: 319 Lexington Blvd; open 9am–5pm daily; $25.99 adults, $14.99 children aged 4–12; www.pearlharbor aviationmuseum.org

Pacific Fleet Submarine Museum: 11 Arizona Memorial Dr; open 7am–5pm daily; $21.99 adults, $12.99 children aged 4–12; www.bowfin.org

USS Oklahoma Memorial: Via a free 90-minute Ford Island Bus Tour; open 3:15–5pm Mon, Wed & Fri; www.recreation.gov

Pearl Harbor Visitor Center: 1 Arizona Pl; open 7am–5pm; www.nps.gov/perl

Pearl Harbor

"A DATE WHICH WILL LIVE IN INFAMY"

That was how President Roosevelt described December 7, 1941, when Japan made a surprise attack on Pearl Harbor. The bombers crippled US military installations on O'ahu, sinking or severely damaging 18 battleships, destroying or disabling nearly 200 aircraft, and killing 2,390 officers and men. The US officially entered World War II after this event.

6 Pacific Fleet Submarine Museum

Charting the history of the US Navy's Submarine Force, this museum displays exhibits such as authentic missiles, a conning tower, and a World War II submarine.

7 USS Bowfin Submarine

The 312-ft- (95-m-) long *USS Bowfin* explains how the US responded to the attack. Nicknamed Pearl Harbor Avenger, SS-287 narrates tales of wartime patrols and conditions for submariners **(below)**.

8 USS Oklahoma Memorial

Hit by nine torpedoes in the December 7 attack, this battleship sank, and 429 crew were killed. This memorial **(below)** is near the *USS Missouri*.

9 Pearl Harbor Visitor Center

This is the gateway to the offshore memorial. Arrive early: free, timed tickets for the documentary film and boat ride are gone by noon on busy days.

10 Pearl Harbor Visitor Center Museum

Events that lead up to the infamous attacks and the devastating aftermath are explained through photographs and artifacts.

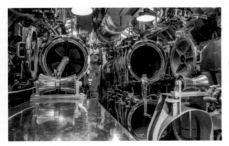

TOP10 ⭐ Bishop Museum

Considered the world's finest museum of Polynesian culture, the Bishop Museum is the designated State Museum for Natural and Cultural History. It is a family-friendly center for scientific and cultural experience and study. It also hosts traveling exhibitions and is home to the J. Watumull Planetarium. Almost every weekend, and on many weeknights, there are lectures, workshops, and openings. The museum also has a fascinating interactive science center.

1 Planetarium
The J. Watumull Planetarium **(below)**, was the first such structure built anywhere in Polynesia when it opened in 1961. It has night-viewing sessions, interactive shows, and the "Science on a Sphere" exhibit in the lobby.

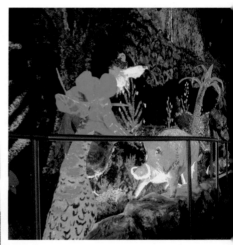

2 Hawaiian Hall
The *koa*-paneled Hawaiian Hall, built in Victorian architectural style and filled with Hawaiian and Pacific artifacts, is the heart of the museum. Spread over three floors, the hall's exhibits focus on Hawaiian religion, royalty and daily life, presenting a modern interpretation of the island's history and culture via some truly stunning collections.

3 Science Adventure Center
Interactive experiences, including erupting volcanoes and deep ocean exploration, are offered at this state-of-the-art center **(above)**.

4 Hawaiʻi Sports Hall of Fame
Honoring Hawaii's athletes, such as Duke Kahanamoku, this exhibit features pictures and memorabilia including Olympic medals.

5 Kāhili Room
This collection **(below)** honors Hawaiian royalty through portraits and displays of royal belongings, including the fragile feather standards called *kāhili*.

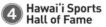

Bishop Museum

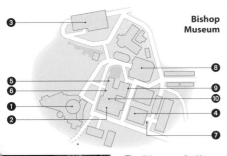

THE AHUPUA'A
Ahupua'a – the small wedge-shaped units of land shown in the Science Garden – were overseen by governors (*konohiki*), who funneled taxes to royalty. The *ahupua'a* encompassed various farming regions and fishing grounds to meet their inhabitants' subsistence needs.

6 Picture Gallery
Considered the world's finest gathering of 19th-century Hawaiian art, the museum's extraordinary collection of oil paintings, watercolors, rare books, and collectibles is on display here.

7 Library
The extensive library within the complex includes a database of published diaries, narratives, and memoirs, all with an emphasis on Hawaiian and Pacific culture.

8 Castle Memorial Building
Dinosaurs, chocolate, and volcanoes have been the subjects of visiting exhibitions held in this building. Most are interactive and aimed at youngsters.

9 Pacific Hall
This was formerly known as the Polynesian Hall, as it focuses on the lifestyle of people across the Pacific. Artifacts such as the carved figures (left), which give an insight into Polynesian rituals, religion, warfare, clothing, music, and dance, are on display here.

10 Joseph M. Long Gallery
This gallery serves as the Bishop Museum's venue for showcasing contemporary Hawaiian art and other items from the museum's collection, including this grass house, or *hale* (below). Special exhibitions are also held here.

NEED TO KNOW
MAP A6 ■ 1525 Bernice St, Honolulu ■ 847 3511 ■ www.bishop museum.org

Open 9am–5pm daily

Adm: $26.95 adults, $18.95 children (aged 4–17) on weekdays; $28.95 adults, $20.95 children on weekends; discounts for seniors, residents, and military.

■ The museum's shop, Pacifica, is one of O'ahu's best gift emporiums. A wide-range of books are available here on topics such as history, archaeology, science, and anthropology.

TOP 10 ⭐ Capitol District

If you had only one day to spend in Honolulu, there's an argument to be made for spending it right here in the Capitol District. Concentrated within a few blocks is a clutch of historic landmarks, a toothsome Asian food market, fragrant *lei* stands, and alluring shops, galleries, and restaurants. And when it's time to sit and contemplate, there's also an ample store of shady mini-parks and cool retreats on hand.

1 US Post Office, Customs House and Court House

Built in 1922, this three-story building is an excellent example of Spanish Colonial Revival architecture. It is also known as the King David Kalākaua Building in honor of King Kalākaua who served as Honolulu's postmaster from 1863 until 1865.

3 Washington Place

Formerly home to Hawaii's governors, this elegant mansion **(above)** has been turned into a museum for Queen Liliʻuokalani, the house's most famous resident.

4 Hawaiian Mission Houses

This living history museum includes one of the earliest examples of American domestic architecture in Hawaii, the coral-block Chamberlain House (1830), as well as two other missionary buildings. There is an excellent gift shop.

2 Hawaii State Capitol

This airy structure **(below)** is imbued with symbolic references to Hawaii. Pools represent the sea, the columns reach up like trees, and the roofline recalls the volcanoes that formed these islands. At the rear of the building is a statue of Queen Liliʻuokalani.

5 St. Andrew's Cathedral

This Gothic-vaulted cathedral took nearly 100 years to build and is the oldest Episcopal edifice in Hawaii. It was consecrated in 1958, upon completion of the final phase of the building's construction.

⑥ Kawaiaha'o Church

"Hawaii's Westminster" **(left)** was built out of 14,000 hand-cut coral blocks. Its name refers to the legend of a sacred chiefess who caused water to flow here, but is also a Biblical reference to "living waters."

Capitol District

⑨ Hawaii State Art Museum

Since 2002, this has been home to a collection showcasing solely the work of island artists.

⑦ Hawaii State Library

With its colonnaded facade, this building is a cool oasis amid the bustle of downtown. The Pacific section is well worth a visit, as is the courtyard.

⑧ Ali'iōlani Hale

The "House of Heavenly Royalty" is the site of the Hawai'i State Supreme Court, and it also houses the free Judiciary History Center. Here, exhibits detail Hawaii's legal history.

⑩ King Kamehameha Statue

During the King Kamehameha Day celebrations each June *(see p64)*, the King Street statue **(below)** is decorated with exuberant *lei* (floral garlands).

KAMEHAMEHA

TOP 10 ⭐ ʻIolani Palace

A National Historic Landmark, this is the only state residence of royalty in the US. It was built for **King David Kalākaua and his queen, Kapiʻolani,** and was the home of his sister, Queen Liliʻuokalani, until her reign ended in 1893. From 1893 to 1968 ʻIolani was the seat of the Hawaiian government. Heavily restored, it includes priceless objects and gorgeous decorative touches.

1 Central Hall and Staircase

This capacious and distinctive hall has doors to the front and back for light and ventilation, and is hung with royal portraits. The impressive staircase **(above)** is the work of royal advisor Walter Murray Gibson.

The elegant facade of Honolulu's ʻIolani Palace

NEED TO KNOW

MAP J3 ▪ Corner of King and Richards Sts, Honolulu ▪ www. iolanipalace.org

Open 9am–4pm Tue–Sat; shop: 8:30am–4pm Wed–Sat; closed public hols

Adm: gallery self-guided tour $26.95 adults, $21.95 teens and $11.95 children; guided tours available

▪ The palace's two gift shops offer a range of interesting souvenirs.

2 Blue Room

In this room, the king received guests informally. A portrait of King Louis Philippe of France dominates; the French were among the countries that considered a closer alliance with the Hawaiian kingdom.

3 Throne Room

The king and queen would sit in state and receive their visitors here **(below)**. In 1895, however, in less happy times for the monarchy, Queen Liliʻuokalani was put on trial in these grand surroundings.

6 Gates and Coat of Arms

The Kauikeaouli Gate, which opens onto King Street, was the ceremonial entrance, used only on state occa-sions. Mounted on its bars is the Hawaiian coat of arms **(left)**; today, some locals wear medallions and amulets emblazoned with this emblem.

7 Sacred Mound

Although most of the royals and chiefs buried here were moved to the Royal Mausoleum in Nu'uanu in 1865, this mound remains an object of respect, as some chiefs may still be buried here.

8 King's Suite

Kalākaua slept in a state bedroom with heavy Victorian furnish-ings, and conducted business and played cards in the library. One of the islands' first telephones is found here.

4 Queen Lili'uokalani's Room

On the second floor is the room where Lili'uokalani was confined for eight months in 1895 after the overthrow of the monar-chy in 1893. The leaders of the coup charged the queen with being involved in an insurrection.

5 Coronation Pavilion

This pavilion was erected for the 1883 coronation of King Kalākaua and Queen Kapi'olani. Embla-zoned with the Hawaiian royal seal, it serves as a bandstand for the Royal Hawaiian Band.

9 'Iolani Barracks

These historic barracks **(below)** now houses the shop, ticket office, and video theater. The shop specializes in designs and patterns inspired by palace ornaments.

10 Palace Galleries

This vast basement complex, with its cham-berlain's offices, servants' quarters, and kitchens, was the heart of the palace. Today, royal treasures are presented here in state-of-the-art displays **(above)**.

TOP 10 ⭐ Chinatown

The first Chinese immigrants came to Hawaii in 1789, followed in 1852 by large numbers who went to work on the plantations. Upon completing their contracts, many opened restaurants and herb shops in downtown Honolulu. After fires in 1886 and 1900, the area fell into disrepair. Today, Chinatown is once again a thriving community where historic shrines stand next to *lei* stands, herbal-medicine shops, farmers' markets, galleries, and restaurants.

① Merchant Street Historic District

South of Chinatown, this district documents the city's commercial development between the 1850s and 1930s, covering a host of architectural styles. It was added to the National Register of Historic Places in 1973.

② Izumo Taishakyo Mission

One of the few active Shinto shrines in the US, this wooden structure **(above)** was inspired by Japan's Taisha Machi shrine. The Hiroshima Peace Bell is on view, and on New Year's Day the shrine is the site of local Shintoists' annual *hatsumōde* (celebration).

③ Open-air markets

Blending Asian and Hawaiian cultures, these vibrant markets **(above)** sell *lei*, traditional clothing, souvenirs, and art. In the morning, stands overflow with fish, meat, noodles, tea, and other delicacies.

④ Honolulu Museum of Art at First Hawaiian Center

This collection of art, in the headquarters of Hawaii's oldest bank, features exhibitions by local artists.

⑤ Honolulu Arts District

On Chinatown's eastern edge, this area is home to cultural institutions, performance venues, and events such as the First Friday Art Walk (5pm, first Fri of month).

NEED TO KNOW

Izumo Taishakyo Mission: **MAP H1** ■ 215 N. Kukui St; 538 7778; open 8am–5pm daily; www.izumo taishahawaii.com

Honolulu Museum of Art at First Hawaiian Center: **MAP J3** ■ 999 Bishop St; open 8:30am–4pm Mon–Fri; www.honolulumuseum.org

Honolulu Arts District: **MAP H2** ■ 1041 Nuʻuanu Ave, Suite B (Downtown Art Center); www.downtown arthi.org

Hawaii Theatre Center: **MAP H2** ■ 1130 Bethel St; 528 0506; www. hawaiitheatre.com

Foster Botanical Gardens: **MAP H1–J1** ■ 180 N. Vineyard Blvd; 522 7066; open 9am–4pm daily; $5, $1 children aged 6–12

Chinatown Cultural Plaza: **MAP H2** ■ 100 N. Beretania St; www.china townculturalplaza.com

■ Tours of Chinatown are available (see pp46–7).

Previous pages Byodo-in Temple in the Kāneʻohe District

REJUVENATION

Chinatown was once home to many gambling parlors and brothels. However, thanks both to its designation as a Historic District in 1973 and to the efforts of its residents and business owners, it has since become a thriving neighborhood filled with art galleries and restaurants.

10 Chinatown Cultural Plaza

With an assortment of restaurants and vendors, the Cultural Plaza is a microcosm of Chinatown. Kung fu and lion-dance performances are held here around Chinese New Year.

Chinatown

6 Festivals

Chinese New Year is celebrated in traditional style (above), while July 4th and New Year's Eve are marked with fireworks. There are also ukulele contests and Cinco de Mayo parties.

7 Dining

Both visitors and Honolulu residents flock to Chinatown to sample the range of Asian food on offer. Vietnamese, Laotian, Chinese, Thai, Japanese, Filipino, and Korean restaurants line the streets, offering a near endless supply of delicious and inexpensive culinary treats.

8 Hawaii Theatre Center

The "Pride of the Pacific" has hosted an impressive array of films and live performances, from local talent to big names. Allow time to explore the atmospheric interior.

9 Foster Botanical Gardens

These beautiful botanical gardens (below) date back to the 1850s. Visitors can explore the gardens on their own, take a guided tour, or try a crafts workshop here.

TOP 10 ⭐ Honolulu Museum of Art

Hawaii's largest fine arts museum, comprising 30 galleries and more than 60,000 works of art, was founded in 1922 by the eclectic collector Anna Rice Cooke, whose home had become crammed with more than 4,500 pieces of art. The gracious stucco-and-tile building, which incorporates Hawaiian, Chinese, and Spanish influences, was erected on the site of Cooke's original house on Beretania Street.

European and American Galleries **1**

This section **(right)** provides a fascinating trip through western art history, with two galleries – Antiquity, and Body and Portraiture – mixing media and eras to reveal how these genres have changed through the centuries.

NEED TO KNOW

MAP M2 ▪ 900 S. Beretania St ▪ www. honolulumuseum.org

Open 10am–6pm Thu & Sun, 10am–9pm Fri & Sat; closed public hols

Adm: $20, aged 18 & under free

Shangri La Museum of Islamic Art, Culture and Design: 532 3685 (to book); tours Thu–Sat (book well in advance); closed Sep; $25; www. shangrilahawaii.org

▪ Tours of Shangri La begin in the Arts of the Islamic World gallery. Following a short film, visitors are transported by van to the museum.

▪ The museum's Doris Duke Theatre hosts independent and international film screenings, concerts, lectures, and performances. For details, call 532 8768.

Shangri La Museum of Islamic Art, Culture and Design **2**

Located in Doris Duke's 1930s-era seaside mansion, this separate branch of the museum features a collection of more than 4,000 objects from Egypt, Iran, and India.

Arts of the Islamic World **3**

In conjunction with the Doris Duke Foundation for Islamic Art, this gallery is made up primarily of pieces from the foundation's broad collection. Furnishings, beautiful woven objects, decorative pottery, and printed papers are all on display.

Arts of Hawaii **4**

This group, which is made up primarily of paintings, graphic arts, decorative arts, and sculpture, includes many of the most recognized artworks in the islands, such as Theodore Wores' famous 1902 painting, *The Lei Maker* **(below)**.

7 Art of the Pacific, Americas, and Africa

Masks, effigies, figurines, religious artifacts, and other pieces from the Americas, Oceania, and Africa are displayed in separate galleries **(above)** and in periodic special exhibits.

8 Henry R. Luce Gallery

This area of the museum incorporates a large space for changing exhibits, the Hawaiian art collection, workshops, and the museum's offices.

10 Southeast Asian and Indian Collections

A gallery of Indian art, mostly collected by a wealthy Indian family who live in Honolulu, has everything from a carved door to wedding attire. Southeast Asian items range from shrouds to sculpture and ceramics **(left)**. Indonesian pieces appear in both the Asian and Islamic collections.

5 European and American Art

Including over 15,000 pieces, this collection is particularly strong in American works in all media and French 19th- and 20th-century painting, such as the Polynesian themes painted by Gauguin.

6 Textiles Collection

Only a fraction of the museum's immense textile collection is on display at any one time. While the focus is on Asia, there are also fine examples of Pacific *tapa* cloth, Japanese *kabuki* costumes, an emperor's *jifu* (robe), and saris.

9 Asian Art Collection

A centerpiece of the museum's Asian holdings is the collection of *ukiyo-e* paintings, which includes *The Great Wave* **(below)**, part of Hokusai's *Thirty-six Views of Mount Fuji*. The collection is also strong in Japanese scrolls and Ming Dynasty paintings.

TOP 10 ⭐ Kalākaua Avenue

Waikīkī's 2-mile- (3-km-) long oceanfront avenue, running from Ala Wai Bridge to the magnificent Diamond Head, is Honolulu's buzzing main strip. Named for Hawaii's playful last king, the street is lined with storied hotels, lively bars and restaurants, a wide variety of high-end shops, parks, and towering palm trees. Its most iconic attraction is Waikīkī Beach, a long arch of soft golden sand and gentle blue waves.

2 Royal Hawaiian Hotel

The "Pink Lady" **(left)** retains her cache. Even if you're not staying at this most famous of Waikīkī hotels *(see p116)*, you can take afternoon tea on the veranda or visit the famed Mai Tai Bar *(see p74)*.

3 Waikīkī Farmers Market

This evening market sets up twice a week on the 1st floor Waterfall Atrium of the Hyatt Regency and features stalls full of locally grown fruit, vegetables, baked goods, and souvenirs.

NEED TO KNOW
MAP G5–M7

Waikīkī Farmers Market: 2424 Kalākaua Ave; 923 1234; open 4–8pm Mon & Wed at the Hyatt Regency Waikīkī Beach Resort and Spa

Honolulu Zoo: 151 Kapahulu Ave; 971 7171; open 10am–3pm daily; $19 ($11 children aged 3–12); www.honolulu zoo.org

Waikīkī Aquarium: 2777 Kalākaua Ave; 923 9741; open 9am–4:30pm daily; $12 ($5 children aged 4–12); www.waquarium.org

■ You can picnic on the grass at Kapiʻolani Park.

1 Moana Surfrider, A Westin Resort & Spa

The porticoed "First Lady" *(see p116)* dates back to 1901. The Sunday champagne brunch is legendary; an evening at the Beach Bar a must.

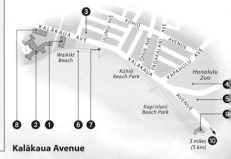

Kalākaua Avenue

HOW TO "GO DIAMOND HEAD"

The extinct Diamond Head volcano crater is such an important icon that Oahuans tell direction by it – "Go Diamond Head" means "Go east" to locals. Hawaiians call the crater "Kaimana Hila" (KYE-mah-na HEE-la), which literally translates as "Diamond Hill." It's also the name of a popular hula.

4 Honolulu Zoo

This compact zoo has a number of warm habitats (see p45). Check out the Komodo dragon. You can also take a backstage zoo-keeper tour or go on a moon-light walk, or an overnight campout.

6 Waikīkī Beach

A lively gathering place, Waikīkī Beach brims with instructors giving surf lessons; locals playing checkers; canoe teams practicing; and locals mingling with tourists in the waves. The whole beach is open to the public **(above)**, including the areas directly in front of the Royal and Moana hotels (see p49).

9 Waikīkī Aquarium

Popular with youngsters for its sharks and turtles, the aquarium is also involved in conservation projects, and hosts reef walks and excursions.

7 Duke Kahanamoku

At Kūhiō Beach, the figure hung with lei **(right)** is Duke Paʻoa Kahanamoku, a pioneer surfer and "Ambassador of Aloha" in the 1960s.

10 Diamond Head

The crater at the end of Kalākaua Avenue **(below)** is two-thirds of a mile across; its brow is 761 ft (232 m) high, and its summit circumference is 2 miles (3.2 km). Take the lovely 0.8-mile (1.2-km) trail to its top to enjoy sweeping views (see p42).

5 Kapiʻolani Park

This 170-acre (69-ha) park was dedicated by King Kalākaua in 1877. It was a military encampment in World War II, but today it is a place for families, music, and festivals **(above)**.

8 Royal Hawaiian Center

This upscale shopping center offers cultural programs such as lei-making and hula lessons.

TOP 10 ⭐ South Shore

Oʻahu's South Shore changes rapidly from suburb to barely touched landscapes of azure bays, botanical gardens, and a shoreline from which whales can be seen in the winter surf. Though close to the city's action, the coast has almost no services – no stores and few restrooms. An occasional food truck at Sandy Beach and a snack stand at Hanauma Bay provide respite.

5 Sandy Beach
Locals love this beach, and on weekends it's busy with body and boogie boarders. Be aware that waves slam into the sloping sand beach with great force, so extra care should be taken.

1 Koko Crater Trail
Strewn with rocks, this abandoned railway track to Koko Crater is one you should approach with caution, good shoes, and a hat.

2 Hanauma Bay
Snorkel in the warm, turquoise waters of this preserve to see delicate coral, vibrant fish **(above)**, and green sea turtles. The central area of the park is the safest; strong currents exist three quarters of the way to either side, ready to surprise snorkelers.

3 Koko Head Trail
This trail involves a ramble along a steep paved road, followed by a scramble along the spine of Koko Head, and then a downhill path for views of the shoreline and the sea *(see p43)*.

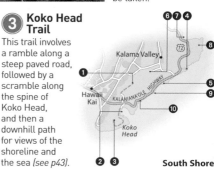

South Shore

4 Wawāmalu and Kaloko
These two beaches are fine for shoreline pleasures, such as sunbathing or flying a kite, but don't even think about taking on the dangerous shore break and swift currents.

KOKO HEAD

The peninsula defining Hanauma Bay is formed out of two volcanic landmarks: Koko Crater and the peak at Koko Head. Koko was the traditional name of a canoe landing at the Wai'alae side of Koko Head. The crater is also called Kohelepelepe. Today, the area is part of a regional park.

6 Koko Crater Botanical Garden

The scent of plumeria flowers (also known as frangipani) is the lasting impression to take away from this dry-land garden **(above)** right inside Koko Crater.

7 Makapu'u Beach Park

One of the top spots in Hawaii for bodysurfing, this beach is best visited during the summer months when the waves are calmer; inexperienced swimmers are advised not to enter the water *(see p102)*.

8 Makapu'u Point Lighthouse Trail

This fairly easy hike along a paved trail leads to a century-old lighthouse *(see p46)*.

9 Hālona Blow Hole

This lava tube **(right)** sucks up water from below as the waves hit the rock, then sends it shooting up *(see p43)*. It is very dangerous to go near the opening; it can be safely viewed from the parking lot.

10 Lanai Lookout

Found along Kalaniana'ole Highway, this roadside lookout offers stunning views across the ocean – on a clear day you might even spot the islands of Moloka'i and Lanai.

NEED TO KNOW

MAP F5–6

Hanauma Bay: 396 4229; open 6:45am–4pm Wed–Sun; $25 adults; www.hanaumabaystatepark.com

Koko Head Trail: the access road is just to the right of the Hanauma Bay entrance

Koko Crater Botanical Garden: 7491 Kokonani St, access via Kealahou St, off Kalaniana'ole Hwy; 768 7135 (for guided hikes); open dawn to dusk daily

■ The Koko Crater Trail starts at the parking lot of the Koko Head District Park at 423 Kaumakani St

■ The South Shore has few services, so make sure to bring beverages and snacks with you.

■ If visiting Hanauma Bay, head out early and reserve your ticket in advance. Parking is limited to 300 spots and costs $3 (cash only). You can rent snorkeling gear at a kiosk by the beach.

TOP 10 ⭐ Kāneʻohe District

The area loosely known as Kāneʻohe is within commuting distance of Honolulu but feels a world away – a gateway to the North Shore and its country-style life. Here, you'll find swathes of farmland, roadside stands selling fresh fish and locally grown produce, and a much slower pace of life. The area is also peppered with historic sites, including fishponds and a temple.

1 Hoʻomaluhia Botanical Garden
The 400 fragrant acres (162 ha) of this park also function as the area's flood-control facility. The botanical garden takes in themed plantings, trails, campsites, a visitor center, and a lake.

3 Kahaluʻu Fishpond
This is one of a handful of working ponds that date from a time when traditional Hawaiians farmed fish using rock walls fitted with *mākaha* (slatted gates) that let fingerlings out but denied escape to larger fish.

4 Haʻikū Gardens
Planted by an Englishman, this park has a small lake, groves of ginger and bamboo, a well-kept lawn, a gazebo, and a pavilion. It is also a popular venue for wedding ceremonies.

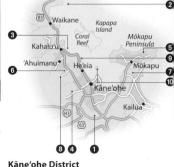

Kāneʻohe District

2 Mokoliʻi
Visible from Heʻeia to Kualoa, this lopsided conical island **(above)** is often visited by kayakers. It is said to be the remains of a giant *moʻo* (lizard god).

7 Kawainui Marsh

Located at the end of Kaha Street, this sizeable wetland *(see p45)* habitat is framed by the Koʻolau Mountain Range. A 1.5-mile (2.5-km) paved trail, much-loved by joggers and cyclists, runs through the marsh **(left)**, allowing you to experience the area's diverse wildlife.

8 Byodo-in Temple

At the rear of the memorial park, this otherworldly structure **(left)** is worth the park admission alone. It's a scale replica of the 900-year-old temple at Uji in Japan, watched over by an immense incense-wreathed Buddha.

9 Heʻeia State Park

With the lush Koʻolau Mountains as a backdrop, this 18-acre (7-ha) property overlooks the calm Kāneʻohe Bay and the ancient Heʻeia Fish Pond. Picnics and weddings are popular here and visitors can also rent kayaks and gear for snorkeling.

5 Mōkapu Peninsula

Visible throughout the district, this peninsula is, alas, out of bounds because it is home to a military base. Despite the hum of aircraft, it is a beautiful sight.

6 Valley of the Temples Memorial Park

This may be a cemetery but it is also a place to take in the islands' cultural diversity and the beauty of the Koʻolau mountains **(below)**. It's common to see families picnicking near the graves of their loved ones; the graves of Buddhists are equipped with food and incense to honor the spirits.

SACRED MŌKAPU

Inhabited as early as the 1st century, the Mōkapu Peninisula was once a farming and fishing area. Hawaiians buried their dead here and built shrines and temples. In the 18th century, King Kamehameha I used the peninsula as a retreat for his aliʻi (chiefs). From 1918, Mōkapu became a US military base.

10 Moku O Loʻe

Tours of Moku O Loʻe are offered by the Hawaiʻi Institute of Marine Biology, which has a research facility on the island. Visitors can learn about the island's history and marine life.

NEED TO KNOW

MAP E4

Hoʻomaluhia Botanical Garden: 45–680 Luluku Rd; 233 7323; open 9am–4pm daily; guided walks 10am Sat & 1pm Sun

Haʻikū Gardens: 46–336 Haʻikū Rd; 247 0605; www.haikugardens.com

Byodo-in Temple: 47–200 Kahekili Hwy; open 8:30am–5pm daily; $5 ,$4 seniors, $2 children aged 2–12; www.byodo-in.com

Heʻeia State Park: 46–465 Kamehameha Hwy; www.heeiastatepark.org

■ Likelike Hwy (H63), the quickest route from Honolulu to Kāneʻohe, offers amazing views. In Heʻeia State Park, you can rent kayaks and snorkeling gear from Kamaʻaina Kayak and Snorkel Eco-Ventures (www.kamaaina kidskayaking.org).

TOP 10 ⭐ Polynesian Cultural Center

Covering 42 acres (17 ha) on O'ahu's scenic north shore, the Polynesian Cultural Center provides an unparalleled opportunity to experience six Pacific Island nations in one place on a single day. Informative and enjoyable, the center has been immensely popular since the 1970s, with nearly one million guests annually.

1 Tongan Village
The only remaining kingdom in the Pacific, Tonga has been ruled by the Tupou family since 950. The Tongan Village features drumming, tapa cloth-making **(above)**, and a nose flute demonstration. Visitors can also try spear-throwing on the village green.

LŪ'AU: A TRADITIONAL FEAST

King Kamehameha II, in 1819, abolished the *kapu* system (religious laws), including a law that men and women had to eat their meals separately. This act spurred the creation of the *lū'au* – a feast shared by a group along with live entertainment. Traditional foods served include *kālua* (roasted pork), *poi* (taro root paste), and *haupia* (coconut milk pudding).

2 Tahitian Village
A French territory since 1842, Tahiti is known for, among other things, its fast, hip-shaking dance, the *tamure*. You can learn the dance at the village **(below)**, but if your hips aren't up to it, you can opt for the coconut bread-making instead.

3 Samoan Village
This village contains replicas of traditional Samoan dwellings – well-built structures made almost entirely from coconut fiber. Here, guests get to learn about Samoan life, including how to open coconut husks with a rock.

Polynesian Cultural Center

NEED TO KNOW

MAP D1 ■ 55–370 Kamehameha Hwy, Lāʻie ■ www.polynesia.com

Open 12:30–9pm Mon–Sat

Adm: adult $79, children $63.96; show packages (which include dinner) start at: adult $139.95, children $111.96; transportation packages also available

■ Hukilau Marketplace is open 11am–8:30pm Monday to Saturday and is free to visit.

6 Huki: A Canoe Celebration

The center's lagoons come alive every day, at 2:30pm, with double-hulled canoes **(left)** filled with dancers and singers in a celebration of thousands of years of legend and lore.

7 Hukilau Marketplace

This 1950s-style outdoor shopping area at the center has souvenir shops, bakeries, and a great selection of restaurants to choose from. Don't miss Tita's Grill food truck for heaps of garlic shrimp and So'Da Bomb for tropical-flavored soda drinks.

8 Hawaiian Village

Hula is one of Hawaii's oldest traditions and this is the place to try the dance for yourself and learn about the symbolism of the moves. At the Hawaiian village, it is also possible to play local versions of bowling and checkers.

4 Aotearoa

Wall carvings conveying ancient stories about the Māori, Polynesian explores who settled in today's New Zealand, are on display here. You can also learn about Māori facial tattoos and watch the *haka* war dance.

5 Hawaiian Journey Theater

The theater features afternoon showings of Hawaiian Experience, a 4-D cinematic extravaganza that puts visitors up close with an erupting volcano, ocean waves, and the beauty of the island.

10 Fijian Village

This village **(below)** features a six-story replica temple known as a *bure kalou* ("spirit house"); it is the only such structure outside of Fiji. Visitors can learn how to make coconut oil and about *kava*, a traditional ceremonial drink.

9 Hā: Breath of Life and the Aliʻi Lūʻau

The former is a lively Polynesian song and dance revue, featuring more than 100 performers; the latter is a *lūʻau*, a traditional feast that's accompanied by contemporary entertainment. Both take place in the Pacific Theater.

The Top 10 of Everything

Vegetation-covered peaks in Hau'ula Forest Reserve, part of the Ko'olau Mountain Range

☰10 Moments in History

1 Formation of the Islands
Each of the islands in the Hawaiian archipelago is actually the top of an underwater volcano. The oldest of the eight major islands (formed some 70 million years ago) is Kaua'i; the youngest is the island of Hawaii, where the active Kīlauea volcano adds more landmass daily.

2 Polynesian Migration
Scholars believe that Marquesan voyagers first came to Hawaii as early as the 4th century, with Tahitians arriving later, in the 13th. It was these two great waves of migration by skilled Polynesian seafarers that first populated the Hawaiian islands.

3 Western Contact
The landing of James Cook, a British captain, at Kealakekua Bay on the island of Hawaii in 1778 is generally acknowledged to be the first time Hawaiians had contact with Europeans. There is evidence that

Statue of King Kamehameha

Spanish ships sailed into island waters in the 16th century, but there are no records of any contact being made.

4 King Kamehameha I Unites the Islands
An accomplished warrior chief from the island of Hawaii, Kamehameha I waged war to conquer O'ahu and Maui, then forced the island of Kaua'i to cede to his dominion. Thus the islands were unified into the Kingdom of Hawaii in 1809.

5 Missionaries Arrive
March 30, 1820 was when the first American missionaries arrived in Hawaii. Over the next 20 years, many more missionaries would follow, taking up residence on all the major islands. They converted many Hawaiians to Christianity, including Hawaiian Queen Ka'ahumanu (1768-1832), and discouraged Hawaiian cultural and religious practices. Their arrival also caused measles and whooping cough to spread through the islands' population.

6 The Plantation Era
From the mid-1800s, American businessmen, who first set up sugarcane production on the Hawaiian islands, started bringing laborers to work the plantations. Work conditions were abhorrent, contracts were akin to involuntary servitude, and camps were divided based on ethnicity. Workers from China were followed by Portuguese, Latin American, Korean, Japanese, and Filipino immigrants. The immigration of those groups led to the multicultural communities found in the islands today.

Painting of James Cook, British captain

7 The Overthrow of the Hawaiian Monarchy

Hawaii was a united, independent kingdom until January 17, 1893, when Lili'uokalani, Hawaii's last queen, was removed from her throne and placed under house arrest in 'Iolani Palace. The coup was the work of American businessmen based in Hawaii. It was not supported by US President Grover Cleveland, who was unable to persuade the provisional government to restore the monarchy. Hawaii was annexed by the US in 1898, and then it became official US territory in 1900.

8 Pearl Harbor Attacked

It was a quiet Sunday morning when Japanese warplanes attacked the US fleet at Pearl Harbor. This attack on December 7, 1941 marked the official entry of the United States into World War II *(see pp12–13)*.

Attack on Pearl Harbor, 1941

9 Statehood

Hawaii became the 50th state in the Union on August 21, 1959. William F. Quinn and James K. Kealoha were sworn in as the new state's first elected governor and lieutenant governor. The occasion is marked each year by a state holiday, Admission Day (third Friday in August).

10 Tourism

Tourists arrived first by ship and then by plane, and by the late 1950s they were visiting in increasing numbers. Today, Hawaii is focused on preserving Hawaiian culture and protecting the islands' fragile ecosystems, while continuing to welcome the huge number of visitors the state receives every year.

TOP 10 HISTORICAL FIGURES

1 Līloa (late 15th century)
One of the first known rulers of the State of Hawaii, Līloa resided in the Waipi'o Valley. His kā'ei (royal sash) is on display at the Bishop Museum.

2 King Kamehameha I (1758–1819)
The ali'i (chief) who in 1809 united the islands into the Kingdom of Hawaii, after defeating Maui's ali'i, Kahekili.

3 Bernice Pauahi Bishop (1831–1884)
The great granddaughter of King Kamehameha I, Bishop was a philanthropist who funded schools and lead charitable organizations.

4 King David Kalākaua (1836–1891)
Also known as the Merrie Monarch, David Kalākaua became king in 1874 and is credited with the revival of hula.

5 Queen Lili'uokalani (1838–1917)
Hawaii's last and one of its most beloved monarchs *(see p19)*. Her government was overthrown in 1893.

6 Duke Paoa Kahanamoku (1890–1968)
The father of modern surfing, Duke was a legendary five-time Olympic medalist who revived the ancient Hawaiian sport of surfing.

7 John Burns (1909–1975)
A statehood advocate, John Burns was elected in 1962 to his first of three terms as governor of the State of Hawaii.

8 John Waihe'e (b.1946)
The first governor of Hawaiian ancestry led the state from 1986 to 1994.

9 Nainoa Thompson (b.1953)
President of the Polynesian Voyaging Society, Thompson helped lead a revival of traditional voyaging arts.

10 Barack Obama (b.1961)
The 44th president of the US, Obama was the first African American president, the first multiracial president, and the first Hawaii-born president.

Queen Lili'uokalani of Hawaii

TOP10 Music and Dance Styles

Hula dancers on Makapu'u Beach

1 Hula Kahiko
In this famous art form, hula dancers are accompanied by percussive instruments made from natural materials and the intonations of one or more chanters. Ancient hula began, it is believed, as a male preserve and as religious ritual.

2 Hula 'Auana
When the practice of hula was revived during the reign of the Merrie Monarch, King David Kalākaua, a new dance style took center stage. Known as *hula 'auana* (modern hula), it is accompanied by instruments such as the ukulele, guitar, standing bass, and singing voices. It is more flowing in style than *hula kahiko*, and dancers generally wear modern clothes.

3 Traditional Hawaiian Chant
As an oral tradition, Hawaiian stories and family histories were related through chant (*oli*). Ranging greatly in style, *oli* are used for many reasons, from prayers and lamentations to requests for permission to gather flora.

4 O-Bon
O-Bon, a traditional Japanese religious observance, has now evolved into a more secular event. O-Bon dances honor deceased ancestors and are joyous occasions marked by drums, music, dances, and, nowadays, festival foods and fun activities.

5 Lion Dance
The Lion Dance is performed all over Hawaii during February's Chinese New Year celebrations. Acrobatic dancers don a lion costume and perform a dance to a steady, loud drumbeat to ward off evil and spread good fortune. Spectators fill red and gold envelopes with dollar bills and feed them to the lion to ensure prosperity.

6 The Sweet Leilani Era
From 1900 to the early 1940s, US mainland composers were greatly influenced by Hawaii, mostly as a result of the way the islands were portrayed by Hollywood. This era – when songs like *Sweet Leilani* and *My Honolulu Lady* were written – is called the *Hapa-Haole* or Sweet Leilani era.

Lion dancers at Chinese New Year

7 Contemporary Hawaiian Music

The renaissance of Hawaiian culture began in the late 1960s and continues to this day, with music playing a major role. The Brothers Cazimero, Ho'okena, the late Israel Kamakawiwo'ole, and Maui's own Keali'i Reichel have combined their voices with modern instruments and classic Hawaiian poetic techniques to create a magnificent new sound.

8 Slack-Key Guitar

The term slack-key refers to a style of playing guitar whereby the strings are loosened, producing a jangly sound. Gabby Pahinui was, perhaps, the most famous of Hawaii's slack-key masters – others included Raymond Kane and Sonny Chillingworth.

Musician playing the slack-key guitar

9 Steel Guitar

The Hawaiian steel guitar was born around the turn of the 20th century, but exactly where, when, and how is still a point of discussion. The instrument is held horizontally on the player's lap, and a sliding steel bar is used instead of fingers on the fret board. The sound was particularly big during the Sweet Leilani era.

10 World Beat

As a miscellany of musical styles from around the world has made its way to the islands, so it is increasingly influencing musicians. Jawaiian describes a blend of reggae and Hawaiian music, and island rappers are now putting their own slant on hip-hop music.

TOP 10 HAWAIIAN MUSIC AND DANCE ESSENTIALS

Traditional hula instruments

1 Pahu
Perhaps the most sacred of hula implements, *pahu* are drums that are traditionally made using coconut tree trunk with a covering of sharkskin.

2 Ipu
A hollowed-out gourd that, in skilled hands, is used to keep the beat in hula.

3 'Ili'ili
Smooth stones – two are held in each hand and played by hula dancers in a style similar to Spanish castanets.

4 Pū'ili
Bamboo sticks, one end of each cut into a fringe so that they produce a rattling sound when played by hula dancers.

5 Kāla'au
Sticks of varying length that are struck against each other during dancing.

6 'Uli'uli
Gourd shakers that are filled with seeds and usually topped with feathers.

7 Ukulele
A gift from the Portuguese that's now integral to modern Hawaiian music. "Jumping flea" was how Hawaiians first described the sound.

8 Guitar
Whether slack-key, steel, acoustic, or electric, the guitar is essential to Hawaiian music.

9 Standing Bass
As in jazz ensembles, the standing bass has found its way into much contemporary Hawaiian music.

10 Falsetto Voice
Most easily described as male vocalists singing above their regular range, there is arguably no sweeter sound than the Hawaiian falsetto.

Traditional Crafts

1 Weaving

Polynesian settlers in Hawaii brought with them the art of weaving. Many of the old everyday objects they created from *lau hala* (leaves of the pandanus tree) and the minutely thin *makaloa* (sedge grass) are considered works of art today. *Lau hala* mats, hats, and bags are easily found in craft shops, but *makaloa* is now quite rare.

Local woman weaving *lau hala* items

2 Lei Making

There's no more enduring symbol of Hawaii than the *lei* (garland). In the past, permanent *lei* were made from shells, seeds, bone, and feathers, and temporary *lei* from vines and leaves. Today, colorful and fragrant flowers such as plumeria and tuberose are most associated with this craft.

3 Heirloom Jewelry

A distinctive style of engraved jewelry, made popular by Queen Lili'oukalani, began in Hawaii in the 1800s. It was inspired by English Victorian gold jewelry adorned with black enamel and carved with floral, vine, and scroll designs. Island jewelers continue to make this style in many different forms.

4 Kapa

Used throughout old Polynesia for clothing, blankets, and decoration, Hawaiian *kapa* is made from the bark of the *wauke*, or paper mulberry tree. The process, which is labor-intensive and time-consuming, involves pounding the bark repeatedly into paper-thin sheets that are then decorated using bamboo tools and plant dyes.

5 Hula Implements

The implements used by hula dancers and their accompanying chanters have changed little over hundreds of years. Though some enthusiasts still craft their own implements, hula supply shops on all the islands now allow dancers to purchase many of the items needed (though the materials used may not always be traditional these days).

6 Quilting

Among the many traditions introduced by the missionaries was quilting. Hawaiians developed their own style of this art form, replacing New England designs with gorgeous renderings of local flora and fauna.

Quilt with the Hawaiian flag and crest

Ukuleles for sale in a shop

7 Ukulele Making

A Portuguese import of the late 19th century, the ukulele quickly found its place in Hawaiian music. Ukulele making is a respected art in Hawaii, and companies like Kamaka on Oʻahu and Mele Ukulele on Maui handcraft high-quality instruments.

8 Featherwork

Cloaks, *lei*, and headware for the *aliʻi* (chief) were all once made with feathers. Birds were trapped so that specific feathers could be plucked before they were released. Yellow, red, and black were the colors most often used. Today, artisans still craft *lei* of feathers from pheasant and other species.

Royal cloak fashioned with bird feathers

9 Fishing Nets

Olonā fiber, derived from a native shrub, was commonly used as early as the 1st century to make fishing nets. Synthetic materials such as nylon replaced *olonā* in the 20th century.

10 Canoe Building

There is a great deal of ritual surrounding the building of a canoe. They are traditionally made of *koa* and always from one log, carefully selected by the boat builder. The craft is still very much alive today.

TOP 10 *LEI* STYLES

1 Haku
Flowers, leaves, or fruit are braided onto three strands of *ti* or other natural fiber. *Haku lei* are most often worn around the head or on a hat.

2 Hili
Hili are braided *lei* made from a single plant material such as *ti* leaf or *maile*.

3 Humupapa
Flowers are sewn onto plant material such as dried banana leaves *(lau hala)*.

4 Kui
This is today's most familiar *lei* and consists of flowers strung together with needle and thread.

5 Kīpuʻu
Long-stemmed leaves or short lengths of vines are knotted together.

6 Wili
Plant materials are attached to a natural backing by winding fiber around them. *Wili lei* have no knots until the very end.

7 Lei Hulu (Feather *Lei*)
Traditionally made of feathers from now mostly extinct or endangered native birds, the art continues using feathers from common birds.

8 Lei Pūpū (Shell *Lei*)
These range from *puka*-shell *lei*, wildly popular in the 1970s, to museum-quality Niʻihau-shell *lei*, worth many thousands of dollars.

9 Seed *Lei*
Simple, single-stranded Job's Tears and intricately crafted *wiliwili*-seed *lei* are popular examples of this type.

10 Contemporary *Lei*
From silk and ribbon to yarn, currency, and even candy, contemporary *lei* are made for every occasion.

Brightly colored *lei*

TOP 10 Natural Wonders

The lighthouse at Diamond Head

1 Diamond Head Crater

This volcanic remnant was named Leʻahi, "brow of the yellowfin tuna," for its shape. Its English name refers to the glinting calcite minerals, which were mistaken for diamonds. The interior has housed military operations and hosted rock concerts. A trail offers sweeping views (see p27).

2 Punchbowl
MAP L1

The 150,000-year-old cone above the city of Honolulu has three iden-tities. Its Hawaiian name, Pūowaina, means "hill of sacrifice" – it was an ancient place of ritual and royal burial. Punchbowl (see p70), its English name, refers to its shape. Today it is also the final resting place of more than 29,000 veterans of American wars in Asia and the Pacific.

3 Waiʻanae Mountain Range
MAP B3–4

Composed of the remnants of the Waiʻanae volcano, said to have become dormant 2.5 million years ago, this range is the higher of the two on Oʻahu, reaching above 4,000 ft (1,219 m). Mount Kaʻala is the highest mountain within this range, and the highest peak on the island; experienced hikers can attempt the slippery 6-mile (10-km), round-trip summit trail. The mountains here have a distinct wet (east) and dry (west) side.

4 Manoa Falls Trail
MAP E5 ▪ End of Mānoa Rd, Mānoa Valley ▪ 587 4175 ▪ Open dawn–dusk daily ▪ www.hawaiitrails. hawaii.gov

A gently sloping but rocky and muddy trail winds through groves of bamboo, eucalyptus, edible mountain apple, and tangled *hau* trees. The 150-ft (46-m) waterfall at the end is spec-tacular after a heavy rainfall. There's no fee for the hike, but parking is $7.

5 Hanauma Bay
MAP F6 ▪ 396 4229 ▪ Open 6:45am–4pm Wed–Sun ▪ Adm ▪ www.hanaumabaystatepark.com

This keyhole-shaped Nature Preserve (see pp28–9) is so beau-tiful and popular that the state has had to restrict access to protect it.

Pristine Hanauma Bay

Tickets need to be purchased in advance, and guests must view a short, mandatory safety orientation video before descending to the bay for snorkeling and sunbathing.

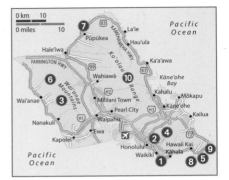

6 Mount Ka'ala
MAP B3

This, the tallest peak on O'ahu at 4,020 ft (1,225 m), is a preserve where indigenous birds and boggy plants prosper in the mist. On its slopes and at its feet, sandalwood once prospered, before the forests were decimated by Hawaiian royalty to pay for Chinese silks and other trade goods.

Bodyboarder at the Banzai Pipeline

7 Banzai Pipeline

Just off 'Ehukai Beach Park, the Banzai Pipeline is the name given to a spectacular winter surf break, the result of a shallow coral reef that serves as a sudden stopping point for deep water currents sweeping inland. The name Banzai comes from the battle cry of Japanese warriors, and was first applied to the waves here during the narration of the late 1950s film *Surf Safari* (see p82).

8 Koko Head
MAP F6

Although not the most impressive peak on O'ahu, Koko' Head's homely bulk is a landmark. Nearby, Koko Crater rises to 1,200 ft (366 m). A panoramic 2-mile (3-km) hike is

reached through a botanical park – the windswept, narrow, and crumbly trail is challenging.

9 Hālona Blow Hole
MAP F5

A lava tube that funnels geysers of sea water high into the air, this dramatic feature is one to observe with care, preferably from the scenic pullout above it. Many who have ventured too near have been injured or killed. From November through March, watch for spouting whales out to sea, as well as spouting water.

10 Ko'olau Mountain Range
MAP C2–D4

The wind- and water-cut Ko'olaus are the subject of countless Hawaiian chants and songs. This Windward-side mountain range (the name means "windward"), so green and dramatic, forms O'ahu's spine from southeast to northwest.

Luxuriant Ko'olau Mountain Range

⏱10 Gardens and Nature Parks

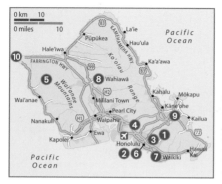

is the oldest botanical garden in Hawaii. It includes some of the oldest trees on the island and endangered tropical plants (see pp22–3).

③ Hawai'i Nature Center

MAP C6 ■ 2131 Makiki Heights Dr, Honolulu ■ 955 0100 ■ www.hawaiinaturecenter.org

This non-profit conservation group encourages children to look after the environment. Weekend family programs – including interpretive hikes, earth care projects, and nature adventures – are held at the center, located in a picturesque ravine in Makiki Valley.

① Lyon Arboretum

MAP C6 ■ 3860 Mānoa Rd, Honolulu ■ 988 0456 ■ Open 9am–3pm Mon–Fri ■ www.manoa.hawaii.edu/lyon

Named for Harold L. Lyon, longtime director of botanical gardens in Honolulu, this university facility is both a field station and a public garden of tropical plants, native plants, conservation biology, and Hawaiian ethnobotany. Classes, workshops, and outings are offered. Admission is by donation and reservations are required.

② Foster Botanical Gardens

Planted by a pioneering botanist in the 1850s, nurtured by an amateur gardener from the 1880s, and donated to the city in 1931, this

④ Moanalua Gardens

MAP D5 ■ 2850 Moanalua Rd A, Honolulu ■ 834 8612 ■ Open 8am–5pm daily ■ Adm ■ www.moanaluagardens.com

This non-profit environmental education center and park in historic Kamananui Valley offers walks and operates an award-winning school program. The free Prince Lot Hula Festival (see p64) takes place each July on a traditional grassy hula pā (mound) in the shady park.

⑤ Mount Ka'ala Natural Area Reserve

MAP B3

This reserve sits alongside a military reservation and is easily reached by road. However, the paved route is off-limits to civilians, who must climb challenging trails to reach the misty bog in a bowl-like hollow atop O'ahu's highest peak. The area has become a safe haven for native plants and wildlife. It's best to consult detailed hiking guides before setting out.

Gazebo in Foster Botanical Gardens

Stream and waterfall in Liliʻuokalani Botanical Gardens

⑥ Liliʻuokalani Botanical Gardens

Bequeathed by the last reigning monarch of Hawaii, this tranquil retreat, devoted entirely to native Hawaiian plants, was established in 1958. The site encompasses portions of Nuʻuanu Valley, including Nuʻuanu Stream and Waikahalulu Waterfall (see p72).

⑦ Honolulu Zoo

The venerable zoological garden in Waikīkī incorporates savanna and tropical forest areas, birds and reptiles of the Pacific islands, and a children's zoo. A summer concert series is hosted here (see pp26–7).

Flamingo at Honolulu Zoo

⑧ Wahiawā Botanical Garden

Opened in 1957, this rainforest garden nestles in 27 acres (11 ha) between two mountain ranges. Used as an arboretum by sugar planters in the 1930s, it is considered the "tropical jewel" of the Honolulu Botanical Gardens (see p93).

⑨ Kawainui Marsh
MAP E4

Rescued from development proposals in the 1960s, this 830-acre (336-ha) wetland (see p31) offers abundant wildlife, including waterbirds, fish, and other aqautic life, as well as archaeological sites. Access is available from a flood control dike.

⑩ Kaʻena Point Natural Area Reserve
MAP A2

Largely unimproved and subject to the pressures of multiple uses such as off-road vehicles, fishers, hikers, shell-collectors, and traditional Hawaiian practitioners, Kaʻena Point park is a narrow strip of land that connects the two ends of Farrington Highway (at Mokuleʻia and Yokohama Bay). Hike a muddy, rutted road, catching sight of small bays and beaches until you reach Oʻahu's end, a tumbled landscape of sand dunes, rocks, and waves (see p47).

Kaʻena Point Natural Area Reserve

ᴛᴏᴘ**10** Treks

Expansive vistas from the Diamond Head State Monument viewpoint

① Diamond Head Trail
MAP C7 ■ The trail begins at the Diamond Head State Monument parking lot, off Diamond Head Rd at 18th St in Kaimukī

Steep in places, dusty and dark in others, this 0.8-mile (1.2-km) paved path *(see p78)* ends in a series of viewing platforms. The landscape before you, from Koko Head in the east to the curve of the Leeward Coast on the west, is worth the energy expended.

Trail leading to Makapuʻu Lighthouse

② Makapuʻu Point Lighthouse Trail
MAP F5 ■ Park at the Makapuʻu Wayside

Makapuʻu Point is the spot where prevailing currents from the deep ocean are split by the land, resulting in interesting wave action. An easy but breezy 2-mile (3-km) walk along the top of a sea cliff leads to a World War II pillbox and Makapuʻu Lighthouse. Watch for whales in winter.

③ Judd Memorial Trail
MAP E5 ■ Reached from Nuʻuanu Pali Drive

This easy one-hour trek in Nuʻuanu Valley is a tribute to the forester Charles S. Judd, who planted the pines here in the 1930s. The pond is less picturesquely named Jackass Ginger after a donkey that used to be tethered in a nearby ginger grove.

④ Makiki Valley Loop Trail
MAP C6 ■ Enter via Hawaii Nature Center, off Makiki Heights Dr

This 2.5-mile (4-km) loop, incorporating short segments of three longer routes – Kaneʻaole Trail, Makiki Valley Trail, and Maunalaha Trail – has been cleared, planted with native vegetation, and equipped with directional signs.

⑤ Honolulu Walking Tours
AIA: www.aiahonolulu.org ■ Hawaii Heritage Center: www.hawaiiheritagecenter.org ■ Historic Hawaii Foundation: www.historichawaii.org/heritagetourism-oahu

The American Institute of Architects (AIA) leads two-hour Saturday tours

(starting at 9am) of downtown Honolulu, taking in examples of various architectural styles. Chinatown tours are led by the Hawaii Heritage Center on Wednesdays and Fridays (9:30–11:30am). The Historic Hawaii Foundation offers free, self-guided tour itineraries that include architectural, cultural, and historical highlights.

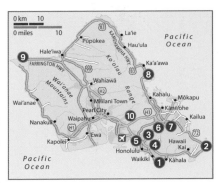

6 Lulumahu Falls Trail

MAP E5 ■ End of Old Pali Rd, off Pali Hwy ■ Open dawn to dusk

This trail that leads to a beautiful waterfall is fairly short (less than a mile) but challenging, and best suited to skilled hikers. The streamside trail is slippery and muddy and takes you through dense bamboo forest, past the Nuʻuanu Reservoir, and close to the ghostly Kaniakapūpū Ruins.

7 Maunawili Trail

MAP F4 ■ Trail starts by the lookout parking area off Pali Hwy

Requiring half a day and someone to pick you up at the end, the Maunawili Trail extends from Pali Highway above Kailua to Waikupanaha Street in Waimānalo. It is a moderately easy 10-mile (16-km) hike for which you will be rewarded with a rainforest valley, then views of the island's windward side.

8 Kualoa Ranch Horse Trails

MAP E3 ■ 49-560 Kamehameha Hwy, Kāneʻohe ■ 237 7321 ■ www.kualoa.com

The Kualoa Ranch (see p98) offers horseback rides at this historic, 4,000 acre (1,619 ha) family ranch dating back to the 1850s. The two-hour rides traverse the base of the Koʻolau Mountains and continue along the wide Kaʻaʻawa Valley.

9 Kaʻena Point Trail

MAP A2 ■ The trailhead is at the Mokulēʻia end of Farrington Hwy

This 5-mile (8-km), two-hour trek along the muddy remains of the shore highway offers pole-fishing sites, shelling in small inlets during low tide, and glimpses of birds, dolphins, and whales (see p84).

10 ʻAiea Loop Trail

MAP D4 ■ From the top of ʻAiea Heights Dr, enter Keaīwa State Park and park at the top

A family-friendly 4.8-mile (7.8 km) hike in and out of the gullies in ʻAiea Valley will familiarize you with vegetation such as ʻuluhe fern and ʻōhiʻa lehua. (Don't pick the scarlet sprays of lehua flowers, local custom says, or it will rain).

Hiking along the Maunawili Trail

TOP10 Beaches

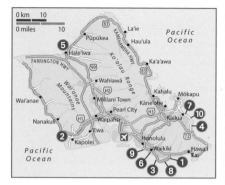

extremely limited, so arrive early or consider taking public transit.

3 Sans Souci
MAP E6

Sprung around a small resort where Robert Louis Stevenson stayed in the 1880s, Sans Souci white sand beach (also known as Kaimana Beach) is good for swimming, body-surfing, and boogie boarding. Safe and shallow, it's popular with families.

1 Wai'alae Beach Park
MAP E6

More popular for weddings and picnics than it is for swimming, this Kāhala beach is hemmed in by coral but offers access to coveted windsurfing areas and fishing holes. Watch out for – and keep small children away from – the deep, sometimes fast-flowing channel cut by Wai'alae Stream as it enters the sea.

2 Ko Olina Beach Park
MAP B5 ■ Kapolei

Four postcard-perfect lagoons fringed by powdery soft sand provide shallow, calm blue waters for swimming and snorkeling. For visitors who are not staying at any of the nearby luxury resorts, parking is

Palm-backed bay in Ko Olina Beach Park

4 Bellows Field Beach Park

Open to the public on weekends and national holidays, this beach park within a military reservation is prized for its broad shelf of powder-fine white sand, turquoise waters, and ironwood-shaded campgrounds (camping is by permit only). It is ideal for swimmers and novice surfers, but watch out for jellyfish *(see p104)*.

5 Hale'iwa Ali'i
MAP B2

This beach park is popular for family picnics, swimming, and surfing offshore at Pua'ena Point. The site has restrooms, a shady pavilion, plenty of food concessions, life-guards, and sports fields, too.

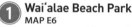

Waikīkī beach, lined with hotels

6 Waikīkī Beach

Possibly the most famous beach in the world, Waikīkī has a lovely beach promenade, an eye-catching waterfall feature, and lush, grassy berms to block street noise. The beach remains prime people-watching territory, as well as being a gentle and safe place for swimming, snorkeling, and learning to surf *(see p78)*.

7 Kailua Beach Park
MAP F4

Around 2 miles (3 km) of golden sand fringe Kailua Bay, which is divided into three sections. The northernmost beaches, Oneawa (with roadside parking) and Kalama (which has a parking lot), are accessed through Kailua neighborhoods. Kailua Beach Park has parking lots, food concessions, a volleyball court, picnic tables, and lifeguard towers. You can surf, windsurf, swim, boat, kayak, canoe, snorkel, and dive here, and the view of Nā Mokulua ("the mokes," as locals call these tiny islets) is the icing on the cake.

8 Ka'alāwai Beach
MAP E6

Reached from a public right of way at the end of Kulamanu Place off Kāhala Avenue and Diamond Head Road, this narrow, white-sand beach is protected by a reef and is safe for swimming and snorkeling. It's also used for diving, pole fishing, and throw-netting, while surfers make spectacular use of breaks in the reef.

9 Ala Moana Beach
MAP B6

This popular beach park in urban Honolulu offers 100 acres (40 ha) for activities, though most people simply swim, wade, and sunbathe on the artificial sandy beach. Visitors must take care, as the channel is deep and, at low tide, swimmers don't have to venture far to be caught in strong currents. Facilities onshore include food concessions, tennis courts, lifeguard towers, and a Biki bike station *(see p111)*.

White-sand Lanikai Beach on O'ahu

10 Lanikai Beach
MAP F4

Frequently voted one of the world's best beaches, Lanikai can be reached through beach access trails in the ritzy Lanikai neighborhood along Mokulua Drive. The beach is flat and sandy, quite narrow in spots, and popular for such activities as swimming, boating, diving, and snorkeling.

🔟 Surfing Beaches

Riding a wave at Point Panic

1 Kaka'ako Waterfront Park/Point Panic
MAP B6

Unless you're highly skilled on a board and ready to join the elite who paddle out to Point Panic every day, this park is strictly for spectators. There's no beach, swimming is dangerous because the break crashes into the retaining wall, and sharks haunt the area. However, a broad pathway extends the length of the park offering great views, and picnic pavilions are clustered along it. This is also a favorite spot for watching celebratory firework displays over Waikīkī.

2 Ala Moana Beach
MAP B6

This area is popular for surfing because it offers a range of challenges from easy and slow Canoes to the more frisky Queen's, Paradise, and Populars areas. Locals who work in Waikīkī hit the waves before and after work.

3 Waimea Bay

Captain Cook first landed on O'ahu at Waimea Bay (see p84). A beach with two personalities, it is calm as a bathtub in summer,

making it ideal for swimming, kayaking, and snorkeling. Come October through to April, it is crowded with open-mouthed visitors watching surfers from around the world ride the wild surf.

4 Sunset Beach
MAP C1

In winter, this wide golden strand is piled high, forming a steep, natural amphitheater for watching surfers attack the awesome waves. In summer, changing tides flatten the beach out, making it more sunbather-friendly. All year long, though, dangerous currents make swimming risky. There are park facilities across the street.

Stretch of golden sand at Sunset Beach

5 Makapu'u Beach Park
MAP F5

The slow rolling shoulders of the waves and the lack of a reef below make this spot (see p103) ideal for bodysurfing. Board surfing is prohibited to prevent collisions. Watch out during high winter surf, and heed flag warnings from the lifeguards.

6 'Ehukai Beach Park

MAP C1

'Ehukai ("sea spray" in Hawaiian) is safe for swimming during spring and summer, but in fall and winter the board surfers take over and it becomes the viewing stand for observing the action at the famous Banzai Pipeline to the left of the beach park.

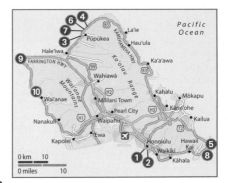

7 Banzai Pipeline

A shallow coral reef extending out from the beach fronting Ke Nui Road throws up waves of tremendous power and steepness – so powerful that no one thought they could be ridden until the 1960s. Injuries from wiping out on the reef are numerous, but surfers can't resist these monsters. "Banzai" was the final battle cry of Japanese kamikaze pilots *(see p82)*.

8 Sandy Beach

"Sandy's" *(see pp104–5)* is the bodyboarding capital of O'ahu and is popular with surfers. Unfortunately, it is also the site of many serious accidents and frequent rescues. A steep drop-off at the sand's edge means that waves are always pounding here, so only the most experienced should take on this surf, and everyone should take care of the treacherous backwash, which frequently catches waders off-guard.

9 Ka'ena Point State Park

MAP A2 ■ Reached via a 2.5-mile (4-km) walk

Until the introduction of tow-in surfing, the mammoth waves of Ka'ena Point remained tantalizingly off limits to surfers because of the impossibility of paddling out from the rock-fringed, current-tossed shore. A north swell at Lae o Ka'ena results in 30–40-ft (9–12-m) waves and brings out the most daring surfers.

10 Mākaha Beach

Site of the Mākaha International Surfing Championships, the beach *(see p93)* here is steep-sloped and wide, with plenty of golden sand and deep waters close to shore. The well-formed waves range from medium in the off-season to very large in the winter. Stray boards can be a hazard to swimmers.

Surfers enjoying the waves at Sandy Beach

Outdoor Activities

1 Gliding and Skydiving at Mokulē'ia

Dillingham Airfield past Waialua on Farrington Hwy, Rte 930, at Mokulē'ia
Air adventures at Dillingham Airfield include gliding, skydiving, and scenic flights *(see p85)*. Choose from a 20-minute single-person glider flight to long scenic flights and lessons.

2 CLIMB Works – Keana Farms

MAP D1 ▪ 1 Enos Rd, Kahuku ▪ 200 7906 ▪ www.climbworks.com
Learn about Hawaii's history and culture while taking in ocean and mountain views during a three-hour zipline tour of a working agricultural farm on O'ahu's North Shore.

3 Jet Skiing at Maunalua Bay

Jet-powered personal watercraft are similar to motocycles and offer a noisy but enjoyable way to skim over the water. By law, jet skis are restricted to weekday, daytime hours. Ask about ski/parasailing combo packages.

4 Guided Hikes

Three non-profit groups – the Sierra Club *(www.sierracluboahu.org)*, The Nature Conservancy *(www.nature. org)*, and Hawaiian Trail and Mountain Club *(www.htmc1910.org)* – offer hikes, with the last group definitely on the hardier side.

Parasailing over the sea at Waikīkī

5 Parasailing at Waikīkī

Hundreds of visitors a day experience the thrill of parasailing – sitting, strapped in a harness attached to a parachute, pulled by a boat, high above the waves.

6 Kayaking Kailua and Kāne'ohe

Locals favor kayaking along the Windward Coast, where small islets offer interesting scenery, and there's a popular sandbar in Kāne'ohe Bay. However, many of the islets are bird sanctuaries where landing is prohibited.

Kayaking along the Windward Coast near Kailua

7 Walking Tours

Regular walking tours of downtown, Chinatown, the Capitol District, Waikīkī, and the University campus are offered by various non-profit groups (see pp46–7). Consult the *Waikīkī Historic Trail*, a free map, for self-guided tours.

8 The Lūʻau Experience

Paradise Cove Lūʻau: 92-1089 Alii Nui Drive Kapolei, Ko Olina; www.paradisecove.com ■ Germaine's Lūʻau: 91–119 Olai St, Kapolei; www.germainesluau.com ■ Ahaaina Royal Lūʻau at the Royal Hawaiian Hotel: Waikīkī; open Mon & Thu only; www.royal-hawaiian.com

Many hotels and venues offer visitors the chance to experience a traditional Hawaiian outdoor feast, known as *lūʻau (see p32)*. Some of the best ones are hosted at the Polynesian Cultural Center *(see pp32–3)*.

Biking through lava fields, Kalapana

9 Bike Hawaii

MAP D5 ■ Honolulu area ■ 734 4214 ■ www.bikehawaii.com

Fun, knowledgeable guides lead mountain biking tours through rainforests and valleys, passing waterfalls, villages, and World War II relics. Biking tours can be combined with snorkeling, hiking, and kayaking.

10 Kahuku Farm Tours

MAP D1 ■ 56–800 Kamehameha Hwy, Kahuku ■ www.kahukufarms.com

Historic, century-old Kahuku Farms takes visitors on a tractor-pulled wagon tour through the fields where açai berries, vanilla, honey, papaya, banana, and several other tropical delights are produced. There's a lovely café and shop on site as well.

TOP 10 RENTAL PLACES AND COMMERCIAL TOURS

Kids on stand-up paddle boards

1 Rainbow Watersports
470 4332 ■ www.rainbowwatersports.com
A stand-up paddle surf school.

2 Gunstock Ranch
341 3995 ■ www.gunstockranch.com
Horse and cattle ranch offering horseback riding tours.

3 Skydive Hawaii
637 9700 ■ www.skydivehawaii.com
Flights for experienced and novice skydivers at Dillingham Airfield.

4 Hawaiian Parasail
591 1280 ■ www.hawaiianparasail.com
Daily flights depart from Kewalo Basin. Free pickup from Waikīkī hotels.

5 X-Treme Parasail
737 3599 ■ www.xtremeparasail.com
This company offers parasailing, fishing expeditions, jet ski rentals, and more.

6 H2O Sports
396 0100 ■ www.h2osportshawaii.com
Operator based at Maunalua Bay.

7 Hawaii Water Sports Center
395 3773 ■ www.hawaiiwatersportscenter.com
Offering a variety of rental equipment.

8 Sun and Salt Adventures Hawaii
262 5656 ■ www.sunandsalthawaii.com
Reputable firm on the Windward Coast.

9 Kailua Beach Adventures
262 2555 ■ www.kailuabeachadventures.com
Ideal for surfboard and kayak hire.

10 Sustainable Tourism Association of Hawaiʻi
800 3531 ■ www.sustainabletourismhawaii.org
For certified sustainable tour operators, consult this association.

📱 Golf Courses

The challenging terrain around the 18th hole at Ko Olina Golf Course

1 Ko Olina Golf Course
MAP B5 ▪ 92–1220 Ali'inui Dr, Kapolei ▪ www.koolinagolf.com

This emerald oasis carved out of a dusty plain by designer Ted Robinson is considered one of O'ahu's most challenging and beautiful courses, featuring water features and black swans. Although expensive, it offers plenty of discounts.

2 Royal Hawaiian Golf Club
MAP F4 ▪ 770 Auloa Rd, Kailua ▪ www.royalhawaiiangc.com

Hidden at the base of the Ko'olau Mountains, in the paradise-like Maunawili Valley, this scenic Greg Norman-designed 18-hole golf course features swaying palms, fish-filled ponds and streams, and plenty of challenges. Expect to lose more than a few balls in the ravines and surrounding rainforest.

3 'Ewa Beach Golf Club
MAP C5 ▪ 91–050 Ft. Weaver Rd, 'Ewa Beach ▪ www.ewabeachgc.com

This enjoyable semiprivate course designed by Robin Nelson manages to retain the character of the historic dryland 'Ewa Plain with its *kiawe* trees and preserved archaeological sites. The tight, manicured fairways and ubiquitous bunkers offer a fair challenge-to-reward ratio.

4 Pearl Country Club
MAP D4 ▪ 98-535 Kaonohi St, Aiea ▪ www.pearlcc.com

Established in the 1960s, this 18-hole course overlooks Pearl Harbor and beyond. Monkeypod trees, coconut palms, and Norfolk Island pine grace the grounds. There is also a driving range, practice putting greens, and a good restaurant on site.

5 Hawaii Prince Golf Club
MAP C5 ▪ 91–1200 Ft. Weaver Rd, 'Ewa Beach ▪ www.hawaiiprincegolf.com

Affiliated with the Prince Waikīkī hotel, this Ed Seay and Arnold

Serene Hawaii Prince Golf Club

Palmer-designed course offers 27 subtly challenging holes. The flattish terrain is bedeviled by winds, tight fairways, and lots of water.

6 Pali Golf Course

MAP E4 ■ 45-050 Kamehameha Hwy ■ 207 7099

In the absence of water hazards and bunkers, the challenge of this undulating landscape is wet and often windy weather. But even duffers can enjoy meandering down swale and up hillside on sunny days.

7 The Golf Courses at Turtle Bay

MAP C1 ■ 57–091 Kamehameha Hwy, Kahuku ■ www.turtlebay resort.com

Two courses are showcased on this 880-acre (356 ha) resort on O'ahu's remote North Shore. The George Fazio Course has wide fairways and deep bunkers; the Arnold Palmer Course incorporates a "tropical links" of sun, wind, and sand on the front nine and a forested upland nine on the back.

8 Hawaii Kai Championship Golf Course

MAP F5 ■ 8902 Kalaniana'ole Hwy, Maunalua ■ www.hawaiikaigolf.com

This coastal course is a windswept beauty, with narrow fairways, plenty of sand, and an ocean view from every tee. Be sure to sign your name on the leaves of the *milo* or "message" tree. A shorter Executive Course is also available.

9 Olomana Golf Links

MAP F5 ■ 41–1801 Kalaniana'ole Hwy, Waimānalo ■ www. olomanalinks.com

Though it's called a links, this much-played windward side course is in view of, but not right by, the ocean. It's a pretty place to play golf, with the mountains as a backdrop and network of ponds, but keep your eye on the ball and watch out for the little lakes.

Putting at Ala Wai Golf Course

10 Ala Wai Golf Course

MAP L5 ■ 404 Kapahulu Ave, Waikīkī ■ 733 7387

One of Hawaii's busiest courses is also one of the most loved on the island for its balance of challenge and playability. While tradewinds may beat your ball back and slow play can test your patience, the course is flat and there's not much water.

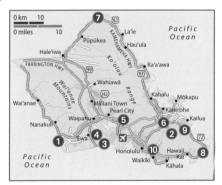

⏱10 Spas and Fitness Centers

A massage cabana at elegant SpaHalekulani

opportunity to work up a sweat. There are two clubs in Honolulu, and five others dotted around Oʻahu; most offer short-term passes.

④ Naupaka Spa
92–1001 Olani St, Kapolei ▪ 387 0308 ▪ www.fourseasons.com

Relax in a private cabin surrounded by foliage at this Four Seasons Resort *(see p116)* spa. Here, a customized Hawaiian flower essence and sea salt blend is made just for you. Treatments also include other Hawaiian-made products such as passion fruit scrubs and macadamia nut oil wraps. There's a fun kids spa menu as well as several salt chambers for halotherapy, too.

① SpaHalekulani
2199 Kālia Rd ▪ 931 5322 ▪ www.halekulani.com

Luxury hotel Halekulani's in-house spa SpaHalekulani uses authentic Polynesian therapeutic rituals with top-notch products and proven techniques. It offers an extensive range of massages, treatments, and hair and nail care services.

② Paul Brown Salon
1200 Ala Moana Blvd #410 ▪ 591 1881 ▪ www.paulbrownsalons.com

One of Oʻahu's top hair salons, Paul Brown has developed a popular line of namesake hair care products that contain Hawaiian plants and sea essences. The salon also offers spa treatments such as classic pedicures.

③ 24-Hour Fitness
951 7677 ▪ www.24hourfitness.com

As the name implies, this national chain offers a round-the-clock

⑤ Heaven on Earth Salon and Day Spa
Bishop Square, 1050 Alakea St ▪ 599 5501 ▪ www.heavenonearthhawaii.com

The place of respite for harried downtown workers is equally agreeable to harried tourists in need of a stress-relieving massage. Owner Lora Nakai wants the feeling of wellness to last, and she encourages therapists to impart helpful tips to clients.

⑥ Unyqe Fitness
745 Fort St ▪ 536 7205 ▪ www.unyqefitness.com

This modern gym offers many services including professionally trained instructors, quality equipment, spa facilities, such as a pool and hot tub, and group fitness classes. Day and monthly passes are available.

⑦ Moana Lani Spa
2365 Kalākaua Ave ▪ 237 2535 ▪ www.moanalanispa.com
Situated inside the beachfront Moana Surfrider, A Westin Resort & Spa (see p116), offers a variety of luxurious treatments, including couples' massages. Relax while taking in ocean views as you sip on champagne.

⑧ HiClimb
826 Ilaniwai St ▪ 888 2999 ▪ www.hawaiiclimb.com
For both beginners and advanced climbers, and everyone in between, this indoor rock climbing gym offers climbing lessons as well as climbing equipment for both rent or purchase. Yoga classes and a weight training room are also available here.

⑨ Marsha Nadalin Salon & Spa
4211 Waialae Ave #5347, Kahala Mall ▪ 737 8505 ▪ www.marshanadalin.com
If chic and upscale Kahala Mall is on your list of shopping stops, you can be rejuvenated at this day spa located in the shopping center. Men's services are available, too.

⑩ Sunset Yoga Hawaii
2735 Kalākaua Ave ▪ 321 3297 ▪ www.sunsetyogahawaii.com
An expert yoga instructor provides group and individual classes on Waikīkī Beach and beyond. All levels are welcome.

Class with Sunset Yoga Hawaii

TOP 10 HEALTH AND BEAUTY TREATMENTS

Pōhaku (stones), used for massages

1 Massage
Shiatsu, Swedish, and Thai styles are available, but why not try Hawaii's traditional *lomilomi* or the newer *Pōhaku* (stone) massage.

2 Steam/Sauna
The steam room is wet, the sauna dry, and either one will open the body's pores in readiness for other treatments.

3 Botanical Baths
Aromatherapy oils, herbs, and seaweeds are added to whirlpool tubs to either calm or re-energize the body.

4 Herbal Scrubs
Scrubs use ingredients such as native red clay and island sea salts to exfoliate, detoxify, and soften the skin.

5 Herbal Wraps
Wraps use a great variety of herbs and the application of heat to draw out impurities from the skin.

6 Facials
Designed to clean and rehydrate the face; choices depend on skin type and individual needs.

7 Aromatherapy
Integrated into many spa treatments, natural fragrances are used to invoke a specific mood or feeling.

8 Manicure/Pedicure
The perfect way to end a day at the spa, manicures and pedicures always include a quick hand and/or foot massage.

9 Makeup
Every salon has experts on hand for a professional application of makeup.

10 Fitness
All gyms and many spas have work-out machines, free weights, pools, and fitness classes.

Local Dishes

① Kālua Pork

The centerpiece of any *lū'au*, or feast, is a whole pig, slow-roasted (*kālua*) in an underground oven. The meat literally falls from the bones. This cooking method also works with turkey, squash, and sweet potatoes.

Hawaiian *poke* bowl with raw tuna

② Sushi, Sashimi, and Poke

The primary Japanese culinary influences are sashimi (sliced raw fish) and sushi (raw fish, shellfish, or vegetables, served on top of, or rolled with, rice). *Poke*, the Hawaiian word for diced or chopped, is Hawaii's version of Latin American *ceviche*. These delicious raw fish-based dishes are available everywhere – from fine dining restaurants to local supermarkets to road-side food trucks.

③ Poi

The staple of the traditional Hawaiian diet, *poi* is made by pounding the corm of the *taro* or *kalo* plant to a paste. Traditional Hawaiians believe their culture to be descended from a *kalo* plant, signifying the symbolic importance of this food.

Kimchi

Introduced by Hawaii's Korean immigrants, *kimchi* is fermented, seasoned cabbage, and for those diners who love sour, spicy, and umami flavors, it is a must try. Traditionally, the cabbage is stored in tightly sealed jars and buried in the ground, then dug up as and when needed.

⑤ Portuguese Sweet Bread and Bean Soup

Fresh from the oven and slathered with creamy butter is the best way to enjoy this wonderful bread, introduced by Hawaii's Portuguese immigrants. Originally baked in outdoor brick ovens, it is now available at markets throughout the islands. Many families in Hawaii have their own Portuguese bean soup recipe. Brimming with beans, meat, and vegetables, it can be a hearty meal in itself, especially when accompanied by a thick slice of sweet bread.

Plate Lunch

Meat, two scoops of rice, and macaroni salad are the three essential elements of the plate lunch. Sold on almost every street corner in Hawaii, it represents the melding of cultures. The meat comes in many varieties, from teriyaki beef to pork and chicken prepared in various ways.

A classic Hawaiian plate lunch

Saimin, a noodle dish similar to ramen

7 Noodles and Rice

Few meals in Hawaii are served without either rice or noodles. Noodles in hot broth with pork and green onions is a common dish for breakfast, lunch, or dinner, and leftover dinner rice often reappears as fried rice for the next day's breakfast.

8 Tropical Fruit

Mango, papaya, guava, *liliko'i* (passion fruit), bananas, and, of course, pineapple. Pure and simple, fresh from the tree, blended into a delicious fruit smoothie, or transformed into an amazing dessert, these are truly heavenly flavors.

Pineapple smoothie

9 Shave Ice

It has other names in other places – snow cone is one – but it is simply small chips of ice, flavored with one or more of myriad syrups, served in a paper cone. Cool and refreshing on a hot summer day, the rainbow variety shave ice has become a virtual symbol of Hawaii.

10 Spam

One of the most maligned foods in history is one of Hawaii's most beloved. Canned Spiced Ham (SPAM) was a military staple because it can be kept for long periods of time. It is, perhaps, the large military presence in Hawaii that first accounted for its curious popularity in the islands.

TOP 10 LOCAL FOOD STOPS

1 Little Village Noodle House
MAP H3 ▪ 1113 Smith St, Honolulu
The menu here offers a full range of northern Chinese specialties.

2 Gulick Delicatessen
MAP D5 ▪ 1512 Gulick Ave, Honolulu
The quintessential plate-lunch eatery.

3 Side Street Inn
MAP E6 ▪ 1225 Hopaka, Honolulu
After-work hangout of Honolulu's chefs, offering savory bar food.

4 Kaka'ako Farmers Market
MAP G6 ▪ 919 Ala Moana Blvd
Shop for locally grown produce and freshly made treats every Saturday, from 8am to noon.

5 Helena's Hawaiian Food
MAP D5 ▪ 1240 N. School St, Honolulu
Helena's has made some of the best traditional Hawaiian food since 1946.

6 Tokkuri-Tei
MAP M7 ▪ 449 Kapahulu Ave, Honolulu
A Japanese *izakaya* (tavern) with an innovative East-West menu.

7 Liliha Bakery
MAP B6 ▪ 515 N Kuakini St, Honolulu
Sample some of the best cream puff pastries, cakes, and pies at Liliha.

8 Palace Saimin
MAP G1 ▪ 1256 N. King St, Honolulu
Serving Hawaii's favorite comfort food: steaming bowls of noodles.

9 Zippy's Restaurants
This chain of O'ahu-style diners serves simple, hearty food (see p107).

10 Rainbow Drive-In
MAP E6 ▪ 3308 Kanaina Ave, Honolulu
This has long been a popular spot for plate lunches and Hawaiian staples.

Neon sign at the Rainbow Drive-In

Restaurants

1 **Lucky Belly**
The Asian fusion menu at this modern ramen joint *(see p75)* is full of decadent and mouth-watering options. Japanese whisky and sake connoisseurs will not be disappointed by the selection available, either. Feeling hungry at 2am? Try Lucky Belly's late-night window for satisfying and surprisingly refined *pūpū* (appetizers).

2 **Mud Hen Water**
Local celebrity chef Ed Kenney serves up an eclectic range of Japanese, Chinese, and Korean dishes with locally sourced ingre-dients at this restaurant *(see p75)*. For brunch, the corned beef and *kalo* (taro) hash is a great option, as is the beet *poke* with avocado and smoked macadamia nuts. The wild Moloka'i venison is a favorite from the dinner menu.

3 **Sansei Seafood Restaurant & Sushi Bar**
Sushi bar, fine dining restaurant, fashionable cocktail lounge, karaoke palace – Sansei Seafood Restaurant & Sushi Bar *(see p81)* is all of these. The name means "third generation" and implies the East-West sophistication that the grandchildren of the immigrant generation have achieved.

Large sushi rolls at Sansei

The chic interior of Koko Head Café

4 **Koko Head Café**
At this café, *(see p107)* Chef Lee Anne Wong creates rich breakfast dishes with Hawaiian and Asian flare – omelettes with miso-smoked pork and onion, bibimbap (mixed rice) with sausage and ham, and volcano eggs topped with spicy tomato sauce, cheese, and vegetables.

5 **The Lanai at Ala Moana**
This modern, open-air food court *(see p75)* at the Ala Moana Center has plenty of great choices for breakfast, lunch, and dinner. Top picks include Musubi Café Iyasume for savory Japanese snacks, Ahi & Vegetable for fresh *poke* bowls, and BRUG for Japanese pastries.

6 **Mahina & Sun's**
Elegant island cuisine made with organic, local, and sustainably sourced ingredients features on the menu here *(see p81)*. The vintage-inspired decor, from the wallpaper

to the furniture, is also locally sourced. Sit poolside for nightly live music and tiki cocktails.

7 La Mer
Hawaii's best and most authentically French restaurant makes lavish use of both local seafood and imported delicacies to create "cuisine de soleil," a cuisine of the sun with a distinctly Provençal bent. Formal dress is required *(see p81)*.

8 The Pig and the Lady
A former pop-up and farmers' market stall, this family-run Vietnamese eatery *(see p75)* in Chinatown serves delicious comfort food with a modern twist. Try the LFC (chicken wings), the Pho French Dip, and, for dessert, the house-special decadent Sundae Funday.

10 DK Steak House
The Waikīkī Beach Marriott hosts a steakhouse *(see p81)* experience that rivals any in the state, complete with in-house dry aged beef and a unique wine list. When you reserveask for a balcony table to enjoy breathtaking views of Waikīkī Beach while you dine.

9 Roy's Restaurant
Roy Yamaguchi founded the first O'ahu restaurant of note in 1988. Here *(see p107)* he offers the same spicy mixture that is his sig-nature – creative cuisine influenced from around the Pacific Rim.

The outdoor area at Roy's Restaurant

TOP 10 REGIONAL INGREDIENTS

Papayas and lychees at a market

1 Tropical Fruit
Chefs make excellent use of pineapple, papaya, guava, *liliko'i*, and lychee in salsas, sauces, and desserts.

2 Local Greens
Small farms grow dozens of varieties of lettuce and greens for use in the restaurants of Hawaii.

3 Vine-Ripened Tomatoes
Much juicier and tastier than their mainland cousins. Growers on all the islands in Hawaii now nurture this important ingredient.

4 Taro
Known as *kalo*, this purple root vegetable has been a staple food on the islands for centuries. Find it in stews, puddings, breads, and as *poi* – a fermented paste.

5 Local Fish
Myriad varieties of local fish, including *moi, mahimahi, ahi, opakapaka,* and *onaga*, form the basis of Hawaii cuisine.

6 Moloka'i Sweet Potatoes
With their brilliant purple flesh, these wonderful potatoes add flavor and color to dishes.

7 Corn
Chefs delight in using sweet, locally grown corn – both white and yellow corn is cultivated in the islands.

8 Slipper Lobster
Smaller than their Maine cousins; it is the sweet tail meat that is prized most.

9 Pohole
These bright green, crunchy, and delicious ferns grow in East Maui and are often served with tomatoes.

10 Local Meat
Beef, lamb, even elk and venison are produced by Hawaii ranches and used extensively by local chefs.

⓾ Honolulu and Oʻahu for Free

Concert by the Royal Hawaiian Band

① Royal Hawaiian Band Concert
MAP J3/M7 ▪ 768 6677 ▪ www.rhb-music.com

Founded in 1836, the Royal Hawaiian Band is the oldest municipal band in the US. Watch them perform on Fridays on the grounds of the ʻIolani Palace (see pp18–19) and at other locations around Honolulu from Wednesday to Sunday.

② US Army Museum
Housed inside Battery Randolph, an old gun battery at Waikīkī Beach, this museum displays films, artifacts, and documents relating to the military history of pre-Imperial Hawaii, World War II, the Vietnam War, and the Korean War (see p77).

③ USS Arizona Memorial
Nearly two million visitors a year take the boat ride to this emotive World War II memorial. The short film and informative audio tour add to the humbling experience.

Tickets are free but must be reserved ahead of your visit, either online for a small fee or at the on-site visitors center (the former is recommended) (see pp12–13).

④ Hoʻomaluhia Botanical Garden
Visitors can go bird-spotting at this large, free to visit botanical garden (see p30) – look out for bright red cardinals, steel-blue Java finches, and spotted nutmeg mannikins in the grassy areas. The garden also hosts numerous workshops including a free drawing and painting session every Tuesday from 9:30am to 12:30pm.

⑤ Royal Hawaiian Center Classes
MAP J6 ▪ 2201 Kalākaua Ave ▪ 922 2299 ▪ www.royalhawaiiancenter.com

From Monday to Friday, this shopping mall offers one-hour cultural classes, including ukulele playing, *lei* making, hula dancing, and weaving. Spaces are limited and are allocated on a first-come, first-served basis.

⑥ Manoa Falls Trail
A 1.6-mile (2.6-km) round-trip through the misty Manoa Valley rainforest leads to a waterfall and back. The Night Marchers (spirits of ancient Hawaiian warriors) are said to haunt these historical hunting grounds. The hike is free, but the parking lot at the entrance of the trail costs $7 (see p42).

Visitors at the USS Arizona Memorial

7 Farmer's Market KCC
MAP C7 ■ 4303 Diamond Head Rd ■ 848 2074 ■ Open 7:30–11am Sat ■ www.hfbf.org

Vendors gather at the Kapiolani Community College to sell flowers, vegetables, fruit, plants, coffee, honey, nuts, meat, seafood, and crafts. Parking fills up fast, so consider taking a bus instead.

8 Koko Crater Botanical Garden

Wander through a dry crater housing a significant collection of drought-tolerant, rare, and endangered plant species from Hawaii and around the world (see p29).

Cacti, Koko Crater Botanical Garden

9 The Hawaii State Art Museum

Three gallery spaces showcase unique and local fine art and craftwork, both contemporary and historical. The sculpture garden, shop, and café are splendid, too. Free hands-on art activites and entertainment for all the family make this museum particularly popular (see p17).

10 Nuuanu Petroglyphs
MAP B6 ■ 2233 Nuuanu Ave

Behind the 19th-century Nuuanu Memorial Park and Mortuary, a grassy trail leads down to a stream and three protected petroglyph sites. Etched onto large boulders centuries ago, the petroglyphs depict mostly human and dog-like figures. There are two small but pretty waterfalls along the trail as well.

TOP 10 BUDGET TIPS

1 Travel during the low seasons
Flights and accommodation prices will be at their most reasonable during April, May, September, and October.

2 Consider staying in a condo
Save money by cooking your own meals in self-catering accommodation.

3 Forgo the beachfront location
Choosing a hotel that is not directly on the waterfront (or a room without sea views) will save you money.

4 Time it right
Look for early-bird dinner specials and happy-hour offerings. *Keiki* (kids) often get discounted menu items, too.

5 Use local transportation
All-day passes for O'ahu's public transportation system cost a mere $7.50.

6 Swim, hike, and walk
Most beaches in O'ahu are public and free to explore, as are many hiking trails, lookouts, and parks.

7 Discover wildlife without a guide
Sea turtles, monk seals, dolphins, and whales can be spotted at places such as Lanikai Beach, Electric Beach, the Hālona Blowhole, and Makua Beach.

8 Go on a self-guided tour
Download the free map of downtown Honolulu from the Historic Hawaii Foundation (www.historichawaii.org).

9 Be entertained on Waikīkī Beach
On Friday nights, starting at around 8pm and depending on the weather, the Hilton Hawaiian Village puts on a fireworks show.

10 Eat local
Browse fresh fruit and traditional food items at one of the island's weekly farmers' markets (www.hfbf.org).

Fruit stalls in Chinatown

⑩ Festivals

Vibrant parade celebrating Chinese New Year in Honolulu

① Chinese New Year
Early Feb

The sound of hundreds of thousands of firecrackers, the time-honored Lion Dance, and bountiful feasts mark Chinese New Year in the islands. Anyone can take part.

② Honolulu Festival
Mar ▪ www.honolulu festival.com

Thousands are drawn to this three-day event that celebrates the diverse cultures of the Pacific Rim. Expect to see a grand parade with performances, live music, a craft fair, food stalls, games for kids, and fireworks.

Clowns at the Honolulu Festival

③ Lei Day
May 1st

"May Day is Lei Day" are the lyrics of a popular Hawaiian song. Not that anyone in the islands needs an excuse to make, wear, or give a *lei*, but May 1st is the day when master *lei* makers showcase their skills.

④ Lantern Floating Ceremony
Last Mon in May ▪ www.lantern floatinghawaii.com

People flock to Ala Moana Beach Park each Memorial Day for the setting adrift of thousands of lanterns to remember those who lost their lives in conflict.

⑤ King Kamehameha Day Celebration
Jun 11th ▪ www.sfca.hawaii.gov

The highlight of the events marking the King's birthday is Oʻahu's colorful Floral Parade, which wends its way through Honolulu and Waikīkī, ending at Kapiʻolani Park. Other activities include concerts, block parties, and an international hula competition.

⑥ Prince Lot Hula Festival
Third Sat Jul ▪ www.moanalua gardensfoundation.org

Held at Moanalua Gardens, this is the oldest non-competitive hula event in Hawaii. It is named for Prince Lot, who reigned briefly as King Kamehameha V and was known for his commitment to the perpetuation of Hawaiian culture.

(7) Hawaii State Farm Fair
Mid-Jul ▪ www.hawaiistate
farmfair.org

Perennial favorites at this fair are the Country Market, which sells produce from island farms, the 4-H Livestock Exhibition, and the Plant Sale.

(8) Aloha Festivals
Mid-Sep ▪ www.aloha
festivals.com

Hawaii's multicultural heritage is celebrated during these festivities, which begin on Oʻahu and move through the island chain with at least a week-long celebration at every stop. There are floral parades, concerts, and craft fairs.

Floral parade at Aloha Festivals

(9) Hawaii Food and Wine Festival
Early Nov ▪ www.hawaiifoodandwine
festival.com

Culinary masterminds from around the globe participate in this week-long gastronomic festival held in Oʻahu. It celebrates Hawaii's abundance of seafood, beef, and poultry with wine tastings, dinners, and special events.

(10) Honolulu City Lights
Dec ▪ www.hnlcitylights.com

In early December the switch is flipped that lights the city Christmas tree and signals the start of the Honolulu City Lights Electric Parade.

TOP 10 SPORTS EVENTS

1 Sony Open
This prestigious PGA tournament is played in January at Waialae Country Club in Honolulu.

2 Great Aloha Run
Tens of thousands run the 8-mile (13-km) race near downtown on President's Day (Feb), many for charity.

3 Transpacific Yacht Race
Better known simply as the Transpac, this sees yachts race from the California coast to Hawaii every other July.

4 Duke's OceanFest
This ocean sports competition is held throughout Waikīkī during the last week of August.

5 Nā Wahine O Ke Kai/Molokaʻi Hoe
First the women in late September, then the men in mid-October paddle outriggers across the island channels.

6 UH Sports
Locals go hog-wild over the amateur volleyball, football, and other games held at the University of Hawaiʻi in winter.

7 Outrigger Rainbow Classic Basketball Tournament
A holiday tournament features the University basketball team competing against its mainland counterparts. It is held at SimpliFi Arena (usually Nov).

8 Vans Triple Crown of Surfing
Professional surfers from all over the world gather on the North Shore in November/December.

9 Hawaiʻi Bowl
Two top-ranked college football teams compete around Christmas in sunny Honolulu at Ching Athletics Complex.

10 Honolulu Marathon
In December some 30,000 runners enjoy Oʻahu's scenic course.

Runners at the Honolulu Marathon

Honolulu and Oʻahu Area by Area

Tranquil Hanauma Bay, home to
a remarkable underwater park

🔟 Honolulu

Hawaii's capital is a wonderfully vibrant and cosmopolitan city. Set along a natural harbor and trimmed by a series of enticing sandy beaches, Honolulu has a host of historical sites, intriguing museums, fantastic restaurants, and boutiques. As the sun sets, the city's Chinatown lights up with busy bars and lounges where locals mingle. Honolulu is also a convenient jumping-off point for plenty of adventures around the island, including waterfall hikes, snorkeling tours and inter-island cruises.

Lei-adorned statue of Liliʻuokalani

Honolulu's Royal Mausoleum

① Royal Mausoleum
MAP B6 ■ 2261 Nuʻuanu Ave ■ 587 2590 ■ Open 8am–4:30pm Mon–Fri

The mausoleum contains the bones of Hawaiian royalty except for Kamehameha I, who was interred in an unknown Hawaii Island location in accordance with custom, and King Lunalilo, whose grave is at Kawaiahaʻo.

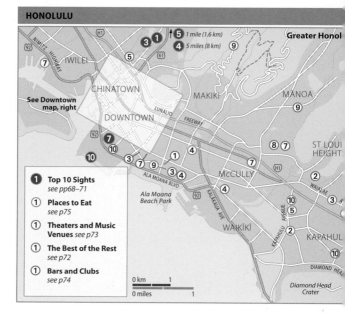

HONOLULU

- ① **Top 10 Sights**
  see pp68–71
- ① **Places to Eat**
  see p75
- ① **Theaters and Music Venues** see p73
- ① **The Best of the Rest**
  see p72
- ① **Bars and Clubs**
  see p74

0 km   1
0 miles   1

② Statue of Lili'uokalani
MAP J3

Weighted with *lei* (garlands) and symbolism, this exceptionally life-like bronze sculpture of Hawaii's last queen stands on the south grounds of the State Capitol *(see pp16–17)*. In her hand she holds a copy of her evocative composition *Aloha 'Oe*, the 1893 Constitution, and the *Kumu Lipo*, Hawaii's creation story. *Ho'okupu* (gift offerings) are often left here by sovereignty activists who revere this queen, who was forced to give up the monarchy under protest *(see p37)*.

③ O'ahu Cemetery
MAP B6 ■ 2162 Nu'uanu Ave ■ 538 1538 ■ Open 6:30am–6pm daily ■ www.oahucemetery.org

The gravestones of this hillside resting place founded in 1844 read like a who's who of Hawaii history, from the humble to the high-class. Nanette Napoleon, "the cemetery lady," has written a guidebook and leads periodic tours – both are well worth seeking out.

View from the Nu'uanu Pali Lookout

④ Nu'uanu Pali Lookout
MAP E5 ■ Off Pali Hwy

As famous for its hair-ruffling winds as for its blood-soaked history, this vantage point is where Kamehameha I fought the final battle with O'ahu warriors *(see p36)*. The latter either jumped to their deaths or fought until they were pushed over the cliff edge rather than give in. This atmospheric site is sometimes cold and misty, but always spectacular.

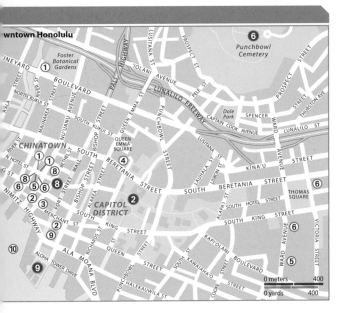

⑤ Queen Emma Summer Palace

MAP C5 ▪ 2913 Pali Hwy ▪ 595 3167 ▪ Open 10am–3:30pm Tue, Thu–Sat ▪ Adm ▪ www.daughtersofhawaii.org

Hānaiakamalama, a modest white, wood-frame house with high ceilings and deep porches, was the perfect warm-weather retreat, just far enough up the Nuʻuanu Heights from Honolulu to catch chilly breezes. Queen Emma (née Rooke), who married King Kamehameha IV in 1856, inherited the home from her uncle. The palace was slated for destruction in the early 1900s, but was saved by the Daughters of Hawaiʻi organization, who now operate it as a museum.

Queen Emma Summer Palace

⑥ Punchbowl Cemetery

MAP L1 ▪ 2177 Puowaina Dr ▪ 532 3720 ▪ Open 8am–6pm daily ▪ Veterans of American Legion members lead free tours

Among Oʻahu's most visited sites, the National Memorial Cemetery of the Pacific, spectacularly situated inside a volcanic crater, offers its visitors

Aerial view of Punchbowl Cemetery

THE CITY'S BEGINNINGS

According to Hawaii's oral history, a Polynesian settlement stood on the site of Honolulu in the 12th century. From the 1700s, the area's calm harbor began attracting merchant ships eager for trade and King Kamehameha I subsequently moved his royal court here in 1809. In 1845, Honolulu became the capital of the Hawaiian Kingdom.

---

extraordinary views and a humbling sense of the human sacrifice brought about by the various wars in the Pacific.

⑦ Kakaʻako Murals

MAP G5 ▪ SALT at Our Kakaʻako: 691 Auahi St ▪ www.saltatkakaako.com

Stroll around the neighborhood of Kakaʻako to find a colorful surprise around every corner. Huge murals decorate industrial warehouse doors, forgotten alleyways, and large brick walls. New murals are added every year as part of the POW!WOW! Hawaii annual festival. Start your street art scavenger hunt at the SALT At Our Kakaʻako shopping mall, which has some stunning murals of its own.

⑧ Nuʻuanu Cultural District

MAP H2 ▪ Between Nimitz and Beretania, River and Bishop Sts

Also known as Gallery Row, this area is made up of a collection of art galleries selling traditional and modern Hawaiian paintings, textiles, and glass, and restaurants, theaters, bars, and nightclubs. The best time to get a sense of its rich life is on the

first Friday evening of each month, when galleries and boutiques hold the First Friday Gallery Walk and stay open until 9pm, offering wine and *pūpū* (snacks), music, and opportunities to meet the artists.

The imposing Aloha Tower

⑨ Aloha Tower
MAP H4 ■ 1 Aloha Tower Dr, Honolulu Harbor ■ 544 1453 ■ Opening times vary, check website ■ www.alohatower.com

This landmark building functions as an integral part of Hawai'i Pacific University, with residences, classrooms, restaurants, services, several shops, and spaces for community events. The ten-story tower, built in 1926 and standing at 184 ft (56 m), was once the tallest building in Hawaii. Today, visitors can take an elevator to the top floor for stunning views.

⑩ Kaka'ako Waterfront Park
MAP B6

On the waterfront, between Sand Island and Ala Moana Beach Park, Kaka'ako Waterfront Park offers grassy knolls, picnic pavilions, and walking and biking paths. It also has views from 'Ewa to Diamond Head, and you can watch the surfers up close at the infamous Point Panic.

MORNING IN CHINATOWN

▶ EARLY MORNING

Chinatown is best enjoyed right after breakfast, when the stands overflow with locally grown fruits and vegetables, imported Asian goods, Pacific fish, freshly made noodles, and every possible part of the chicken and pig. Wear comfortable shoes, dress for sunshine, and park at one of the less expensive municipal lots on Smith or Maunakea Streets.

The area between River and Nu'uanu, Beretania and King is great for small gifts – sandalwood soap, painted fans, kitchen tools, dried persimmons, Chinese pottery, and red-and-gold good-luck banners. You can watch the butchers chop *char siu* (barbecue pork) with incredible speed and skill and buy some fresh fruit from one of the market stalls.

LATE MORNING

When you're ready, head *mauka* (toward the mountains) on River Street until you meet up with North Vineyard Boulevard. There you'll find the gorgeously arrayed **Kuan Yin Temple** *(see p72)* and cool, green **Foster Botanical Gardens** *(see p44)*. Explore these before returning to Chinatown for lunch.

Try one of the popular restaurants in the Chinatown area, such as **Cuu Long II** (Vietnamese on N. Hotel), **Fook Lam** (dim sum on N Beretania Street), **Little Village Noodle** House (Chinese on Smith Street), **Pho To Chau** (*pho* soup on River Street), or **Sing Cheong Yuan Bakery** (savory *manapua* barbecue pork buns on Maunakea Street).

See map on pp68–9 ←

The Best of the Rest

1 Kuan Yin Temple
MAP H1 ■ 170 N. Vineyard Blvd
■ 533 6361 ■ Open daily

Light bounces off the exterior of this Chinese place of worship; inside, incense drifts and the goddess of mercy looks on as devotees pray.

Exterior of the Kuan Yin Temple

2 Alexander & Baldwin Building
MAP H3 ■ 822 Bishop St

This 1929 four-story terracotta-and-tile A&B building epitomizes Territorial period Hawaiian architecture. Asian, Mediterranean, and island influences have been combined by architects C.W. Dickey and Hart Wood.

3 Ala Moana Center
MAP B6 ■ 1450 Ala Moana Blvd
■ www.alamoanacenter.com

With more than 350 stores and regular live entertainment, this is the world's largest, open-air shopping mall.

4 Ala Wai Canal
MAP G5–M6, G6

With a wide path along its entire length, the canal offers a lovely evening's walk, ending at the Ala Wai Yacht Harbor.

5 Liliʻuokalani Botanical Gardens
MAP B6 ■ 123 N Kuakini St, Honolulu
■ 522 7066 ■ Open 7am–5pm daily

This garden (see p45) was a retreat for the queen, where she picnicked to the sounds of Nuʻuanu Stream.

6 Honolulu Museum of Art School
MAP B6 ■ 1111 Victoria St ■ www.honolulumuseum.org

This center sees exhibitions and sales of various art societies.

7 Japanese Cultural Center of Hawaiʻi
MAP C6 ■ 2454 S Berentania St
■ www.jcch.com

Exhibits on the history of Japanese immigration to Hawaii since the 1860s are on display at this center. Classes in tea ceremonies and martial arts are hosted here as well.

8 University of Hawaiʻi
MAP B6 ■ www.hawaii.edu

Two self-guided walking tours focus on the campus's plant life and art work.

9 Tantalus Drive
MAP E5

The loop drive from Makiki Street up Round Top Drive, and along Tantalus Drive is not to be missed – picnic along the way at Puʻu ʻUalakaʻa Park.

10 Honolulu Harbor
MAP G3–H3 ■ Honolulu Fish Auction: www.hawaii-seafood.org

Almost all of the state's waterborne traffic passes through here. Early birds should check out the Honolulu Fish Auction tours that take place at the harbor around 5:30am daily.

Skyline around the Honolulu Harbor

Theaters and Music Venues

A Motown tribute act at The Republik

1 The Republik
MAP M4 ▪ 1349 Kapiolani Blvd
▪ www.jointherepublik.com

This trendy event space hosts international DJs, 80s bands, and tribute acts. Under-18s require an adult to accompany them to the concert hall. Its adjoining lounge, The Safehouse, serves great food and drinks.

2 Mamiya Theatre
MAP C7 ▪ 3142 Wai'alae Ave
▪ 739 4886

Mamiya, named after the surgeon who funded it, is a space used for recitals, dance, and performances.

3 Kumu Kahua
MAP H3 ▪ 46 Merchant St
▪ www.kumukahua.org

This 100-seat experimental theater focuses on new cutting-edge work from around the Pacific.

4 Tenney Theatre
MAP J2 ▪ 229 Queen Emma Sq
▪ www.htyweb.org

The Tenney is a small performance center that hosts the Hawaiian Theatre for Youth.

5 Neal S. Blaisdell Arena
MAP L3 ▪ 777 Ward Ave
▪ www.blaisdellcenter.com

When Honolulu hosts a rock show or sports competition, this mid-century modern, circular hall is where it happens.

6 Neal S. Blaisdell Concert Hall
MAP L3 ▪ 777 Ward Ave
▪ www.blaisdellcenter.com

This concert hall is home to the Honolulu Symphony, the Hawai'i Opera Theatre, Ballet Hawaii's annual holiday *Nutcracker*, and most other symphonic events.

7 Kennedy Theatre
MAP B6 ▪ 1770 East-West Rd, UH campus ▪ 956 7655

The campus theater has a 600-seat main theater and the smaller Earle Ernst Lab Theatre. The season includes plays and musicals, and Kabuki and Noh Japanese dramas.

8 Hawaii Theatre Center
MAP H2 ▪ 1130 Bethel St
▪ www.hawaiitheatre.com

A former movie theater, the wonderfully renovated Hawaii Theatre Center offers a full and varied season, from *hula hālau* fundraisers to visiting dance companies.

The Hawaii Theatre Center at night

9 Manoa Valley Theatre
MAP B6 ▪ 2833 E. Mānoa Rd
▪ www.manoavalleytheatre.com

This small but highly respected theater in a former church hall stages plays and musicals.

10 Diamond Head Theatre
MAP C7 ▪ 520 Makapu'u Ave, Kaimukī ▪ www.diamondhead theatre.com

This community theater features musicals, comedy, and contemporary drama productions.

See map on pp68–9 ←

Bars and Clubs

 Manifest
MAP H2 ■ 32 N. Hotel St
■ www.manifesthawaii.com
Modern coffee shop by day, and trendy lounge by night, this Chinatown hangout is a favorite see-and-be-seen spot among the city's sophisticates.

 Murphy's Bar and Grill
MAP H3 ■ 2 Merchant St
■ 531 0422
Downtown watering hole that offers a taste of Ireland; it also hosts one of the Pacific's largest St. Patrick's Day celebrations.

3 **WorkPlay**
MAP G5 ■ 814 Ilaniwai St
■ 457 1322
Sip cocktails out on the patio or settle down with a craft beer, and enjoy the nightly live music at this cozy café-style bar. Sophisticated, private themed-rooms can be reserved.

 Mai Tai's
MAP B6 ■ Ala Moana Center
■ 941 4400
Very much a local favorite, this bar has live Jawaiian (local reggae) music, comfortable couches, and a relaxed lounge style.

 Smith's Union Bar
MAP H2 ■ 19 N. Hotel St
■ 538 9145
A down-and-dirty dive bar that has been serving cheap drinks to a wide mix of customers since 1934. It hosts karaoke every night.

 The Dragon Upstairs
MAP H2 ■ 1038 Nuʻuanu Ave
■ 526 1411
Some of the city's top jazz musicians gather at this intimate Chinatown hideaway to jam through the night, much to the delight of music lovers.

 Hana Koa Brewing Co.
MAP B6 ■ 962 Kawaiahao St
■ 591 2337
Located in a former Coca-Cola factory, this craft brewery offers a choice of 18 beers alongside smoked marlin toast and pickled onion rings.

 The Tchin Tchin! Bar
MAP H2 ■ 39 N. Hotel St
■ 528 1888
Visit on the first Friday of the month (for First Friday Art Gallery Walk), and this wine and cocktail bar, along with all the other bars in this part of Chinatown, will be full of jovial locals.

9 **Bar Leather Apron**
MAP H3 ■ 745 Fort St
■ www.barleatherapron.com
This stylish speakeasy whisky bar offers creative, well-balanced concoctions. Score one of the six seats at the bar for top-notch service.

10 **Moku Kitchen**
MAP G5 ■ 145-660 Ala Moana Blvd ■ 591 6658
A modern, urban restaurant, Moku Kitchen gets lively in the evenings with music. Pick your libations from a selection of craft beers, wines, and unique cocktails. Happy hour runs from 2pm to 5:30pm.

Band jamming at the Mai Tai's

Places to Eat

1 Lucky Belly
MAP H2 ▪ 50 N. Hotel St
▪ 531 1888 ▪ $

It's not just the ramen that draws a nightly crowd to this Chinatown joint (see p60). Try the equally tempting oxtail dumplings and the *kochujang* brisket *bibimbap*.

2 Uncle Bo's
MAP M7 ▪ 559 Kapahulu Ave ▪ 735 8310 ▪ $$

Uncle Bo's is one of Waikīkī's most popular late-night spots for wildly creative appetizers and social snacks. The modern, casual environs attract a hip clientele.

3 Mud Hen Water
MAP C7 ▪ 3452 Waialae Ave ▪ 737 6000 ▪ $$

A bright, friendly space (see p60) where farm-to-table dishes include sourdough banana pancakes, veggie congee, savory fern shoots, and fried chicken.

4 Sushi Sasabune
MAP B6 ▪ 1417 S. King St ▪ 947 3800 ▪ $$$

The *omakase* menu here is justly famous, with perfectly seasoned bites, from oysters to octopus to abalone, scallops, *ahi*, and more. Reservations are a must at this superb venue.

5 Ono Seafood
MAP M7 ▪ 747 Kapahulu Ave ▪ 732 4806 ▪ $

Tiny takeout spot for fresh and healthy *poke* bowls (raw diced fish salad) where you get to pick the fish, rice, sauce, and toppings.

6 The Pig and the Lady
MAP J3 ▪ 83 N. King St
▪ 585 8255 ▪ $$

Traditional family recipes combined with innovative cooking skills make up the Vietnamese dishes at this welcoming restaurant (see p61).

7 Nico's Pier 38
MAP H3 ▪ 1129 N. Nimitz Hwy
▪ 540 1377 ▪ $$$

Lyon-born chef Nico Chaize creates gourmet dishes using market-fresh fish in a relaxing waterfront location with indoor and outdoor seating. There is also a bar and a fish market.

Whole fried fish with a tomato salad

8 Moke's Bread & Breakfast
MAP C7 ▪ 1127 11th Ave ▪ 367 0571 ▪ $

Try the fluffy liliko'i pancakes and *loco moco* (beef patty over rice, topped with fried eggs and gravy) at this diner.

9 The Lanai at Ala Moana
MAP H3 ▪ 1450 Ala Moana Blvd, Ala Moana Center ▪ 955 9517 ▪ $

An airy, stylish food court perfect for grabbing a quick bite – sushi, burgers, and stir-fried dishes are all on offer here at the various kiosks.

10 Leonard's Bakery
MAP M7 ▪ 933 Kapahulu Ave
▪ 737 5591 ▪ $

This beloved local bakery specializes in *malasadas* (Portuguese doughnuts).

See map on pp68–9 ⬅

TOP10 Waikīkī

Previously a bucolic farming area and the site of King Kamehameha I's rural summer bungalow, Waikīkī is now one of the city's busiest areas. Watched over by Diamond Head Crater, this resort neighborhood is famous for its golden beach, lapped by turquoise waters and fringed by palm trees, luxury hotels, and buzzing restaurants. Nearby, great shopping is on offer at both the modern International Market Place and bustling Kalākaua Avenue.

Sun-seekers on palm-lined Kūhiō Beach Park

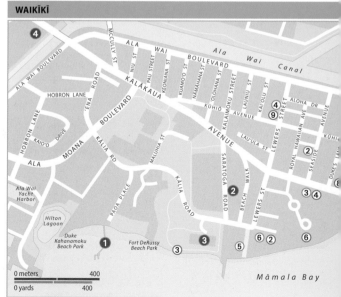

WAIKĪKĪ

1 Atlantis Submarines Waikiki

MAP H7 ▪ 252 Paoa Pl ▪ 973 9800 ▪ Open 7:30am–6pm daily ▪ www.atlantisadventures.com

Those who want to venture under water to view sea life without all the gear and training can join an eco-tour via a battery-powered submarine. Air-conditioned vessels dive to depths of up to 100 ft (30 m). Through large windows, you can see green sea turtles, stingrays, sharks, yellow tangs, and other underwater marine life.

Tank in the US Army Museum

2 Urasenke Tea House

MAP J6 ▪ 245 Saratoga Rd ▪ 923 3059 ▪ Donation

Teaching Cha-do, the Way of Tea, a ceremony meant to both relax and focus the mind, is the mission of this center endowed by the Urasenke Foundation in Kyoto. Public demonstrations are offered weekly, and private ones can be arranged by calling ahead.

3 US Army Museum

MAP J7 ▪ Battery Randolph, 2131 Kālia Rd, Fort DeRussy ▪ 438 2819 ▪ Open 10am–5pm Tue–Sat ▪ www.hiarmymuseumsoc.org

This well-designed free museum celebrates the US Army's multi-faceted history in the Pacific. It covers Hawaii's "Go for Broke" 100th Infantry Battalion, Waikīkī as a Vietnam War R&R center, and more *(see p62)*.

4 Hawaii Convention Center

MAP G5 ▪ 1801 Kalākaua Ave. ▪ 943 3500 for tour info ▪ Open 8am–5pm weekdays ▪ www.meethawaii.com

A contemporary masterpiece of glass and soaring white columns, the Convention Center, across the Ala Wai bridge from Waikīkī proper, was dedicated in 1998 and contains dozens of artworks and more than a million square feet of meeting space. The venue hosts an array of events and performances including the Honolulu Festival and the Honolulu Mineral, Fossil, Gem & Jewelry Show.

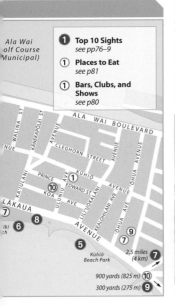

Ala Wai Golf Course (Municipal)

1 **Top 10 Sights**
see pp76–9

1 **Places to Eat**
see p81

1 **Bars, Clubs, and Shows**
see p80

ALA WAI BOULEVARD

WALINA ST · KANEKAPOLEI ST · CLEGHORN STREET · KAIULANI AVENUE · PRINCE EDWARD ST · KOA AVE · ULUNIU AVE · KUHIO AVENUE · KEALOHILANI AVE · OHUA AVE · KAPAHULU AVENUE

LĀKAUA · AVENUE

7 6 8 5 9 7 9 10

Kūhiō Beach Park

2.5 miles (4 km) 7
900 yards (825 m) 10
300 yards (275 m) 9

The Hawaii Convention Center

5 Kūhiō Beach Park
MAP L7

Once known as Hamohamo, this area was the location of Pualeilani, the beach home of Queen Kapiʻolani and later her adopted son, Prince Jonah Kūhiō Kalanianaʻole, a delegate to the US Congress. During his lifetime he opened the beach near his home to the public, and left it to the city when he died.

View from the Diamond Head Crater

7 Diamond Head Crater
MAP C7 ■ Open 6am–6pm daily (last entrance 4pm) ■ Adm ■ Credit cards only, reservations required

Watching over Waikīkī, Diamond Head Crater's sculpted slopes are shadowy green in rainy season and a dusty parched brown at other times. In addition to the summit trail within the crater, a 4-mile (6.5-km) loop walk allows you to see the peak from a full circle. Start where Monsarrat Avenue meets Diamond Head Road and proceed in either direction.

8 Kahuna (Wizard) Stones
MAP L7 ■ Kūhiō Beach, Kalākaua Ave

The four large slabs at Kūhiō Beach represent four mysterious historical figures called *Kapaemahu* ("people of a changeable nature"). These people came from Tahiti and taught the art of healing to the Hawaiians. The stones were erected in their memory and have occupied various locations, but are currently gathered at the beach formerly known as Ulukou.

Surf tables for rent at Waikīkī Beach

6 Waikīkī Beach
MAP L7

Waikīkī Beach *(see p49)* is possibly the most famous strip of golden sand in the world. It has a lovely promenade, an eye-catching water-fall feature, and flower-filled grassy berms to block street noise. Often busy, the beach is lined with hotels and oceanside bars, and is a great – and safe – place for swimming, snorkeling, and learning to surf.

9 Kapiʻolani Bandstand
MAP C7 ■ Kapiʻolani Park

The current, vaguely Victorian stone structure – a spacious circular stage with a peaked roof held up by a

series of pillars – is the fourth incarnation of a bandstand first built in the 1880s. It is a popular venue for concerts and is often used for informal jam sessions.

⑩ International Market Place

MAP K6 ■ 2330 Kalākaua Ave ■ Open 11am–9pm daily ■ www. shopinternationalmarketplace.com

First opened in 1956, International Market Place reopened as a modern shopping, dining, and entertainment center in 2016 after extensive renovations. Free festivities, performances, and myriad artisan stalls ensure that even the youngest shopper is kept entertained.

Entrance of International Market Place

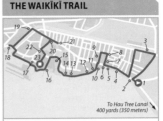

To Hau Tree Lanai
400 yards (350 meters)

▶ MORNING

Take a self-guided tour along the Waikīkī Historic Trail that is maintained by the Native Hawaiian Hospitality Association. Be sure to stop at each historic trail marker to learn about the area's rich history. Visit the trail website *(www.waikikihistorictrail. org)* for a free trail map.

The trail was the brainchild of the late visionary George S. Kanahele, a pioneer of cultural tourism. It's marked by a series of sculpted surfboards imprinted with photographs, maps, and information at 20 locations around the neighborhood.

Most hikers begin at the first marker on Waikīkī Beach at the site of the Outrigger Canoe Club, founded in 1908 to promote surfing, canoe paddling, and other activities.

Stopping points include a former residence of Queen Liliʻuokalani; the villa of Chun Afong, who was Hawaii's first Chinese millionaire; the vast coconut grove of Helumoa; and a war camp of Kamehameha I.

LATE MORNING

The tour lasts about an hour-and-a-half, after which you have plenty of time to stroll some more or do some shopping.

Stop for lunch at the **Hau Tree Lanai** *(see p81)* in the Kaimana Beach Hotel at the east end of Waikīkī. Here you can sit at the exact spot where Robert Louis Stevenson enjoyed the shade under the hau tree in 1893 as he penned stories about the South Pacific.

See map on pp76–7

Bars, Clubs, and Shows

Colorful dining room under a bamboo-and-grass roof at Duke's Waikīkī

1 Duke's Waikīkī
MAP K7 ▪ Outrigger Waikīkī Beach Resort, 2335 Kalākaua Ave ▪ 922 2268

Named after surf legend Duke Kahanamoku and outfitted with his memorabilia, this popular bar offers food and live music.

2 Lewers Lounge
MAP J7 ▪ Halekulani Hotel, 2199 Kālia Rd ▪ 923 2311

This romantic cocktail lounge has some of the island's leading mixologists and features nightly live jazz.

3 KOA Oasis
MAP H6 ▪ Hale Koa Hotel, 2131 Kālia Rd ▪ 955 0555

Sink your toes into the soft sand with an expensive, delicious mai tai in hand at this beachfront shack.

4 Rock-A-Hula
MAP K6 ▪ Royal Hawaiian Center, 2201 Kalākaua Ave ▪ 629 7458

Tribute artists and local talent stage highly entertaining shows in a 750-seat theater. Options include pre-show drink and dinner add-ons.

5 Hideout
MAP K7 ▪ The Laylow, 2299 Kūhiō Ave ▪ 628 3060

This gorgeous rooftop terrace is surrounded by the Waikīkī skyline and decorated with lush plants. Morning coffees and pool-side cocktails are on offer. Reservations are recommended.

6 RumFire
MAP K7 ▪ Sheraton Waikīkī, 2255 Kalākaua Ave ▪ 922 4422

Come here for the outstanding oceanfront views, cozy fire pits, tasty appetizers, and fruity cocktails.

7 The Beach Bar
MAP K7 ▪ Moana Surfrider, A Westin Resort & Spa, 2365 Kalākaua Ave ▪ 922 3111

Quench your thirst at this casual oceanside bar with a lava flow or other tropical cocktails. Nibble on *poke* nachos while enjoying the live music and the evening breeze.

8 Maui Brewing Co.
MAP K7 ▪ Waikīkī Beachcomber by Outrigger, 2300 Kalākaua Ave ▪ 971 4321

Spacious bar with 36 specialty and craft beers on tap. Come during the happy hour, Mon to Fri 3:30 to 4:40pm, for discounted drinks and pizzas.

9 Bacchus Waikīkī
MAP K6 ▪ 408 Lewers St ▪ 926 4167

Cozy LGBTQ+ bar with a welcoming, laid-back vibe and weekly trivia nights.

10 Wang Chung's
MAP L6 ▪ 2424 Koa Ave ▪ 921 9176

This LGBTQ+ friendly nightclub, a popular karaoke spot, offers specialty liquors for those in need of some Dutch courage.

Places to Eat

1 **Me Bar-B-Q**
MAP L7 ■ 151 Uluniu Ave
■ 926 9717 ■ $

Visit this Korean take-out counter for tender barbecued meats, rice, and vegetables – perfect for a picnic at the beach.

2 **Heavenly Island Lifestyle**
MAP K6 ■ Shoreline Hotel Waikiki, 342 Seaside Ave ■ 923 1100 ■ $

Fresh island fruit, honey, and farm eggs are just some of the healthy local ingredients that make up the menu at this brunch diner.

3 **Doraku Sushi**
MAP K6 ■ Royal Hawaiian Center, 2233 Kalākaua Ave ■ 922 3323 ■ $$

Don't let the mall location deter you from visiting this excellent sushi hot-spot with a terrace. Good happy hour.

4 **Mahina & Sun's**
MAP K6 ■ Surfjack Hotel, 412 Lewers St ■ 924 5810 ■ $$

Chef Erik Leong elevates Hawaiian cooking here (see pp60–61), with dishes such as chicken payaya soup, shrimp étouffée, and oxtail risotto.

5 **La Mer**
MAP J7 ■ Halekulani Hotel, 2199 Kālia Rd ■ 923 2311 ■ Open D only ■ Formal attire necessary ■ $$$

Savor each bite while watching the sun set at this fine dining French gourmet restaurant (see p61).

6 **House Without a Key**
MAP J7 ■ Halekulani Hotel, 2199 Kālia Rd ■ 923 2311 ■ $$$

Named after a novel featuring fictional detective Charlie Chan, this hotel hangout is a sunset favorite for cocktails or casual meals. There is also live music and hula dancing.

7 **DK Steak House**
MAP K7 ■ Waikiki Beach Marriott Resort & Spa, 2552 Kalākaua Ave ■ 931 6280 ■ $$

The steaks and seafood are out-standing here (see p61), as are sides such as the bacon and truffle mac and cheese.

8 **Hula Grill Waikīkī**
MAP K6 ■ 2335 Kalākaua Ave ■ 923 4852 ■ Open B, L & D ■ $$

Regional Hawaiian fare is served along the water's edge, with views of the beach and Diamond Head.

9 **Sansei Seafood Restaurant & Sushi Bar**
MAP K7 ■ Waikiki Beach Marriott Resort & Spa, 2552 Kalākaua Ave ■ 931 6286 ■ $$

Come during happy hour and reserve a spot on the beach-side balcony to enjoy the Japanese fare served here (see p60).

10 **Hau Tree Lanai**
MAP M7 ■ Kaimana Beach Hotel, 2863 Kalākaua Ave ■ 921 7066 ■ $$

Reasonably priced Pacific Rim cuisine is served here beneath the spreading branches of a hau tree.

The sleek, elegant entrance of La Mer

See map on pp76–7 →

TOP 10 North Shore

The North Shore is many things to many people. For big-wave riders, it is the peak of their craft. For Honoluluans, it's rural upcountry, and turning-around point for Sunday drives. And for those who appreciate flavorful food, it's an important source of superb produce – from tropical fruits and coffee to corn and free-range beef. The coastline itself displays a split personality over the course of the year. From April to October, the beaches are playgrounds, broad and golden, visited by gentle waves. From October to April, however, high surf robs them of sand, or piles it high into dunes, and the potential danger of swimming here cannot be overstated.

Surfing at Banzai Pipeline

1 Banzai Pipeline
MAP C1

At ʻEhukai Beach Park, located between Ke Waena and Ke Nui Roads off Kamehameha Highway, expanses of sand fringe a rocky shore, over which the surf boils. The most famous of the wild surfing breaks is the tubular Banzai Pipeline (see p43). Lifeguards are kept very busy here because of the steeply sloping ocean bottom and the irresistible allure of huge winter surf.

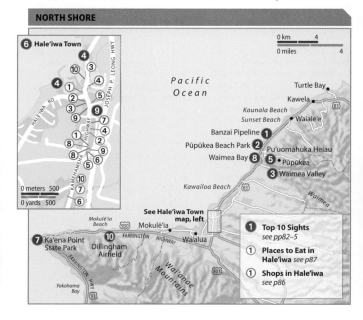

NORTH SHORE

6 Haleʻiwa Town

0 km 4
0 miles 4

Pacific Ocean

Turtle Bay
Kawela
Kaunala Beach
Sunset Beach • Waialeʻe
Banzai Pipeline 1
Pūpūkea Beach Park 2 Puʻuomahuka Heiau
Waimea Bay 8 5 • Pūpūkea
3 Waimea Valley

Kawailoa Beach

0 meters 500
0 yards 500

See Haleʻiwa Town map, left

Mokuleʻia Beach
Mokuleʻia
Waialua
FARRINGTON HIGHWAY
7 Kaʻena Point State Park
10 Dillingham Airfield

Waiʻanae Mountains

Yokohama Bay

1 Top 10 Sights
see pp82–5

1 Places to Eat in Haleʻiwa see p87

1 Shops in Haleʻiwa see p86

Pūpūkea Beach Park, a popular spot for snorkelers and scuba divers

2 Pūpūkea Beach Park
MAP B1

The 80 acres (32 ha) of Pūpūkea Beach Park include two very popular snorkeling and skin-diving areas. Shark's Cove is a rocky inlet, often used by scuba-diving operators for training. Three Tables is a network of shallow coral reefs and ponds. The Pūpūkea Foodland store, across the highway, is great for provisions, and the Sunset Beach Fire Station offers aid and information.

3 Waimea Valley
MAP C2 ▪ 59–864 Kamehameha Hwy, Hale'iwa ▪ 638 7766 ▪ Open 9am–4pm Tue–Sun ▪ Adm ▪ www.waimeavalley.net

Once an adventure park with tram rides and cliff divers, this valley is now owned by Hi'ipaka LLC, a non-profit organization. The center's focus is on the conservation of the valley's natural resources and layered history through interpretive hikes and cultural activities.

4 Hale'iwa Ali'i Beach Park and Hale'iwa Beach County Park
MAP B2

These parks (see p48) flank each other on either side of the Anahulu River, and if they look familiar it's because they were a primary set for Baywatch Hawaii. Ali'i Park features a boat ramp and is popular for fishing and surfing. Across the river, Hale'iwa Beach offers safe swimming and is an excellent place for a family party or picnic.

5 Pu'uomahuka Heiau
MAP C1 ▪ From Kamehameha Hwy, drive up the hill on Pūpūkea Rd; the dirt track into the *luakini heiau* is on the right and is marked by a visitor attraction sign

This *luakini heiau* (sacrificial temple), honoring the war god Kū, is the largest on O'ahu. It encompasses an expansive network of three enclosures that command panoramic views of Waimea Bay and the surrounding countryside. An altar has been restored at which you may see (but not touch) personal offerings.

The historic site of Pu'uomahuka Heiau

THE WILD NORTH SHORE

If you're interested in wildlife, several beaches along this coast serve as basking areas for turtles. Wedge-tailed shearwaters nest in the area during the late summer and fall, and whales can be seen frolicking offshore between the months of November and April.

6 Haleʻiwa Town
MAP B2

Allow a couple of hours to explore historic Haleʻiwa Town, with its eclectic community of surfers, artists, and families who have lived in "the house of the ʻiwa bird" for generations. Once a gracious retreat for wealthy summer visitors, Haleʻiwa Town has a certain timelessness. To get a feel for it, park at either end of town and simply walk around the plantation-era buildings, browsing the shops

Sign for Haleʻiwa Town

and art galleries, and lingering on the Anahulu River Bridge to watch the water flow by.

7 Kaʻena Point State Park
MAP A2

This sprawling state park begins at the abrupt and muddy end of Farrington Highway and takes you along a wild, boulder-strewn shoreline to the dunes at Oʻahu's westernmost tip. This is said to be where the souls of the dead leapt into the afterlife. It's an extremely hot two-hour hike (Kaʻena means "the heat"), but worth it for the beauty of the landscape and the whales you can spot in season. Take sunscreen, a hat, water, and sturdy walking shoes.

8 Waimea Bay
MAP B1

This legendary surf spot *(see p50)* is also a good choice for scuba divers and free divers. It has a wide, sandy beach, which is great for sunbathing. Picnic areas, showers, and rest rooms make Waimea Bay an ideal place to spend the day. In summer the waves subside, and it is possible to swim in the ocean. However, it is important to heed lifeguard warnings. As this is one of the most popular beaches on the North Shore, parking is limited, so get there early.

Golden sand at Waimea Bay

⑨ Lili'uokalani Protestant Church

MAP B2 ■ 66–90 Kamehameha Hwy ■ 637 9364 ■ Open daily ■ www.liliuokalanichurch.org

Queen Lili'uokalani was part of this congregation when she visited her summer home in Hale'iwa. Though the present structure dates only from 1961, a century-old moon-phase clock she gave to the church is proudly displayed. The original church, made of grass *(hale pili)*, was built in 1832 at this site.

Lili'uokalani Protestant Church

⑩ Dillingham Airfield

MAP A2 ■ 69–415 Farrington Hwy, Mokulē'ia ■ 656 1027 ■ Honolulu Soaring: 637 0207; offers daily flights

This airport *(see p52)*, also known as Kawaihapai Airfield, is known as a center for gliding, skydiving, and scenic flights.

NORTH SHORE EXCURSION

▶ MORNING

A 50-mile (80-km) round trip from Waikīkī may not seem that far, but most of the route is on two-lane highways, so you can't rush, and there's a lot to see. As it is a bit too far to drive in one day, it may be worth checking in at Kahuku's **Turtle Bay Resort** *(see pp116–17)*, which offers hotel rooms and spacious suites as well as condos and cottages with full kitchens and multiple bedrooms.

From there, you can drive into **Hale'iwa Town** for a morning shopping spree – some items are cheaper than in the city, notably *pareo* (sarong) wraps. Have lunch at **Kua'aina Sandwich Shop** *(see p87)* or the **Beet Box Café** *(66-437 Kamehameha Hwy)*.

AFTERNOON

For the rest of the afternoon, you can keep going north and take a heart-thrilling glider ride at **Dillingham Airfield** or rent a surfboard from **Surf N Sea** *(see p86)* in Hale'iwa Town. Alternatively, head back toward the Turtle Bay Resort, stopping to enjoy a bit of sunbathing or snorkeling along the way.

Try to plan your excursion around an event – check the Go Hawaii site *(www.gohawaii.com)* for an events calendar in advance of your trip. Highly recommended are the Hale'iwa Farmers Market (Thursday afternoons), the Hale'iwa Art Walk (second Saturday of every month), and the thrilling winter championship surf meets, which aren't always easy to schedule because they are wave-dependent.

See map on p82 ←

Shops in Haleʻiwa

 The Ukulele Site
66–560 Kamehameha Hwy
■ 622 8000

Find ukuleles in all colors and sizes at this little shop. Knowledgeable staff will help you pick the right one and even offer a lesson or two.

2 **The Growing Keiki**
66–051 Kamehameha Hwy
■ 637 4544

For unique, handmade items for kids, check out the eclectic array of funky clothing, books, toys, and gifts at this children's shop.

3 **San Lorenzo Bikinis**
66-057 Kamehameha Hwy
■ 637 3200

This store sells a unique assortment of bikinis, some with daringly cheeky designs. You can mix and match them. They also have beach hats and towels.

4 **Rainbow Bridge Gift Shop**
62–620 Kamehameha Hwy
■ 637 7770

Choose from colorful sarongs, beach towels, ukuleles, and locally made shirts and jewelry, all at fair prices, at this lovely gift shop.

5 **Polynesian Treasures**
66–250 Kamehameha Hwy,
North Shore Marketplace ■ 637 1288

Stacked with unusual designs by more than 50 artisans, handi-crafts shop has carved bone amulets and quilted items.

 Silver Moon Emporium
66–250 Kamehameha Hwy,
North Shore Marketplace
■ 637 7710

An eclectic boutique for women's and children's clothing and accessories. Styles range from breezy beach to city chic. Locally handmade jewelry is also on sale here.

 North Shore Surf Shop
66–150 Kamehameha Hwy
■ 637 5002

Pick up surfing gear and locally designed clothes for the whole family at this well-known shop; surfboard and bike rentals are also available.

8 **Barnfield's Raging Isle Surf and Cycle**
66–250 Kamehameha Hwy, North Shore Marketplace ■ 637 7797

This store has everything for bicycles, including rentals and repairs. You'll also find custom boards by Bill Barnfield and stylish casual wear.

9 **Mahina**
66–111 Kamehameha Hwy
■ 784 0909

A wonderful collection of breezy sundresses, light tops, and trousers in soft fabrics, plus a range of coordinating accessories, is available at this women's clothing store.

10 **Surf N Sea**
62–595 Kamehameha Hwy
■ 637 9887

Established in 1965, this watersports-fanatics' paradise is the oldest surf shop on Oʻahu. It offers everything from swimwear to snorkel tours and kayak rentals. The friendly staff will even fix that ding in your board after you've tackled Waimea Bay.

The venerable Surf N Sea shop

Places to Eat in Haleʻiwa

PRICE CATEGORIES
Price categories include a three-course meal for one, a glass of house wine, and all unavoidable extra charges including tax.

$ under $30 $$ $30–$60 $$$ over $60

 1 **Haleiwa Joe's**
66–011 Kamehameha Hwy
■ 637 8005 ■ $$

With a view of Haleʻiwa harbor from its patio, this friendly open-air restaurant specializes in locally caught, fresh seafood dishes.

2 **Waialua Bakery**
66–200 Kamehameha Hwy
■ 744 1032 ■ $

The excellent smoothies, sandwiches, and cookies keep visitors coming back for more at this bakery, popular with surfers.

3 **Haleʻiwa Beach House**
62–540 Kamehameha Hwy
■ 637 3435 ■ $$

Classic Hawaiian seafood dishes, *pupu* platters, and colorful cocktails are served in this airy spot on the beach.

 4 **Kuaʻaina Sandwich Shop**
60–160 Kamehameha Hwy
■ 637 6067 ■ $

This fast-food eatery is famous for its good-value third-of-a-pound burgers and crisp fries. It also serves gourmet sandwiches and salads.

5 **Shave Ice Stops**
Matsumoto's (66–111 K. Hwy)
■ Aoki's (66–082 K. Hwy)

Two neighboring operations offer sweet, drippy shave ice, a legacy of the days when ice was shipped to Hawaii from Alaska in giant blocks. The shavings, created when the blocks were cut, were treasured by children. In the 1920s, Chinese entrepreneurs made fruit syrups to pour over the ice, and Japanese crafters created a plane-like device to shave it. Pick the shortest line and enjoy the shave ice.

6 **Surf N Salsa**
66–521 Kamehameha Hwy
■ 692 2471 ■ $

Stop by this popular food truck for fresh Mexican food that can be picked up and eaten here or savored at a shaded picnic table.

7 **Giovanni's Shrimp Truck**
66–472 Kamehameha Hwy
■ 293 1839 ■ $

This food truck serves large plates of ridiculously good (if unpeeled) garlic shrimp. Be aware of the long lines.

Crowds at Giovanni's Shrimp Truck

8 **Kono's**
66–250 Kamehameha Hwy
■ 637 9211 ■ $

Try the breakfast bomber burrito or 12-hour braised pork plate, both top picks at this breakfast/brunch spot.

9 **Coffee Gallery**
66–250 Kamehameha Hwy, North Shore Marketplace
■ 824 0368 ■ $

At Coffee Gallery, browse local art while sipping on-site roasted coffee. Try the mocha freeze iced coffee and the house-made granola.

10 **Café Haleʻiwa**
66–460 Kamehameha Hwy
■ 637 5516 ■ $

Mexican-accented lunches preceded by ample breakfasts are the fare at this café, which is open only until mid-afternoon.

See map on p82 ⬅

TOP10 Central and Leeward Oʻahu

If you have the time to venture beyond the glamour of Waikīkī and the allure of the North Shore, Central and Leeward Oʻahu offer the chance to better understand the everyday life of the island – the neighborhoods and shops, the laid-back restaurants, and the lesser-known beaches. ʻEwa, once the quintessential company town, recalls its roots with a reconstructed plantation village. Ko Olina's gentle lagoons and the beaches of Waiʻanae offer great sun and sand time. Several sacred sites – some restored, some mere remnants – remind us of the historical importance of these areas.

Outrigger canoes on the sandy beach at tranquil Pōkaʻi Bay

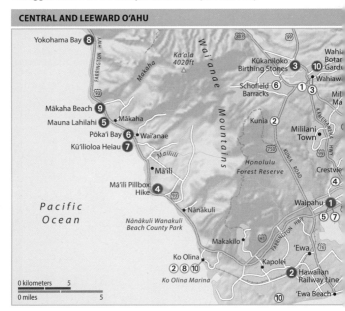

CENTRAL AND LEEWARD OʻAHU

Yokohama Bay 8
Mākaha Beach 9
Mauna Lahilahi 5 • Mākaha
Pōkaʻi Bay 6 • Waiʻanae
Kūʻilioloa Heiau 7
Māʻili
Māʻili Pillbox Hike 4
Nānākuli

Pacific Ocean

Nānākuli Wanakuli Beach County Park

Makakilo

Ko Olina 2 8 10
Ko Olina Marina

Kapolei

ʻEwa

Hawaiian Railway Line 2

ʻEwa Beach 10

Kaʻala 4020ft △

Kūkaniloko Birthing Stones 3
Schofield Barracks 6

Wahiawā Botanical Gardens 10
Wahiawā

Kunia 2

Mililani Town

Honolulu Forest Reserve

Crestview

Waipahu 1
5 7

Waiʻanae Mountains

0 kilometers 5
0 miles 5

Previous pages The Diamond Head crater seen from Waikīkī Beach

Room at Hawaii's Plantation Village

1 Hawaii's Plantation Village

MAP C4 ▪ 94–695 Waipahu St, Waipahu ▪ 677 0110 ▪ Open 9am–2pm Mon–Sat ▪ Adm age 4 & above ▪ www.hawaiiplantationvillage.org

The era when more than 400,000 immigrants from China, Japan, Korea, and the Philippines, as well as Hawaiians, labored on sugar and pineapple plantations is memorialized in the 30 original structures gathered to create this living history museum. Tours are led by volunteers, many of whom are former plantation laborers or descendants of workers.

2 Hawaiian Railway Line

MAP C5 ▪ Catch the train from 91–1001 Renton Rd, 'Ewa ▪ 681 5461 ▪ Train rides: 1pm Wed, noon & 3pm Sat, 1pm & 3pm Sun ▪ Adm ▪ www.hawaiianrailway.com

Starting in Ewa, round-trip train rides on the Hawaiian Railway Line take two hours and stop at Kahe Point and Ko Olina. On board, a narrator tells passengers stories about the sugar cane trains and the sugar plantation history of the area. Afterwards, visitors can drive back to Ko Olina to swim in the artificial lagoons in the shade of coconut palms and then have lunch or dinner at Monkeypod Kitchen (see p95).

3 Kūkaniloko Birthing Stones

MAP C3 ▪ From Kamehameha Hwy heading toward Wahiawā, turn left on Whitmore Rd, then continue to the dirt parking lot and the palm grove

Bloodlines were all-important to ancient Hawaiians. In royal birthing areas like Kūkaniloko, the upright stones served as support for the chiefly mother and also as chairs for the attendant priests and relatives, on hand to testify to the child's royal lineage.

1	**Top 10 Sights** see pp90–93
1	**Places to Eat** see p95
1	**The Best of the Rest** see p94

Ko'olau Range

Kahalu'u

Pacific Palisades

'Ahuimanu

83

Waimalu

Keaīwa Heiau State Park

H3

4 5 6
9 8 9

'Aiea

3 1

Hālawa

Pearl Harbor

7

LIKELIKE HIGHWAY

63

Fort Shafter

Salt Lake

Kailihi

Kapalama

Honolulu ✈

Palama

Hickam

Honolulu

The birthing stones at Kūkaniloko

Beachgoers enjoying the calm coast of Pōkaʻi Bay

4 Māʻili Pillbox Hike

MAP A4 ■ Waapuhi St & Kaukama Rd, Māʻili

Along a hot and dry ridge called Puʻuʻohulu Kai, this moderate, 2-mile (3-km) hike takes about an hour and a half. The trail forks occasionally but all the trails make their way up to the pillboxes (World War II military bunkers) that you can see about half way up. One has been painted bright pink for breast cancer awareness. The view from the top is stunning, with the Ko Olina lagoons towards the south and Mākaha Beach to the north.

5 Mauna Lahilahi

MAP A4 ■ Mākaha

Peaking out of a peninsula in between Makaha Beach and Mauna Lahilahi Beach, this little mountain, only 230 ft (70 m) high, has been a sacred Hawaiian site for centuries. Petroglyphs depicting human and dog-like figures have been found on its eastern side and there are some ancient burial and temple remains scattered about as well.

6 Pōkaʻi Bay

MAP A4 ■ 5–037 Waiʻanae Valley Rd

Beautiful and tranquil, Pōkaʻi Bay Beach Park is one of the most welcoming beaches for swimming and snorkeling along the Waiʻanae Coast. It's safe all year round because of the protection of a long breakwater. The bay's name, "night of the great one," is rooted in the story of a voyager from the south, Pōkaʻi, who is said to have planted the first coconut grove on the island on this site.

7 Kūʻilioloa Heiau

MAP A4

This sacred site on Kāneʻilio Point is believed to have been a blessing point for travelers arriving and departing by canoe. Its name refers to a dog-god who protected voyagers.

KAʻENA FROM THE WEST

Though most folks come to Kaʻena Point from the Mokulēʻia side, the 5-mile (8-km) trek from the Waiʻanae direction offers a sandier section of the old Farrington Highway. En route, watch for yellow *ilima*, purple *pāʻū o hiʻiaka*, and white *naupaka* flowers.

⑧ Yokohama Bay
MAP A3

So-called because of its popularity with Japanese pole fishers, this is the last sandy shore on the north-western coast of O'ahu. It's also part of a large but undeveloped park complex that stretches around the end of the island to Ka'ena. Though known as a popular surfing site, it is also a place where you can enjoy the beach in relative isolation.

⑨ Mākaha Beach
MAP A3 ▪ 84–369
Farrington Hwy

Mākaha (meaning "fierce") lives up to its name, with high surf and a runoff pond behind the beach that periodically breaks through the sand bar and rushes into the bay. In the past, it was infamous for a group of bandits who terrorized the area. Today, with the exception of when the surf is high, it is a safe beach for swimming.

The high surf at Mākaha Beach

⑩ Wahiawā Botanical Garden
MAP C3 ▪ 1396 California Ave, Wahiawā ▪ 621 5463 ▪ Open 9am–4pm daily ▪ Guided tours available

Founded by commercial sugar planters as an experimental arboretum in the 1920s, this rainforest garden has tropical flora that require a cooler climate. The emphasis is on native Hawaiian plants, although there are also many plants from other countries around the world. Many of the older trees date to the 1920s *(see p45)*.

A DAY WITH DOLPHINS

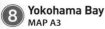

▶ MORNING

Schools of spinner and bottlenose dolphins, and, from November to March, pods of humpback whales are readily seen just off the Wai'anae Coast. Several cruise companies offer dolphin-watching excursions in various crafts, usually with small numbers of passengers. The excursions depart from **Wai'anae Boat Harbor** or **Ko Olina Marina**. Most offer transport from Waikīkī hotels, though you can choose to pick up the tour at the harbor. You will have to get up early, though, because the boats usually depart promptly at 7am. Wild Side Specialty Tours *(306 7273; www.sailhawaii.com)* offers whale and dolphin-watching cruises aboard charter boats and catamarans with marine biologist and research crew members. The boats accommodate a maximum of six passengers and the three-hour tours include snorkeling gear and lunch.

AFTERNOON

After your cruise, head over to **Monkeypod Kitchen** *(see p95)* for lunch – if you time your meal to finish around 3:30pm, you will then be able to catch the happy hour and live-music segment.

Spend the rest of the afternoon watching the green sea turtles at nearby **Paradise Cove Beach**. This is a quiet, pretty spot and it's good for small children, but be aware that there are no lifeguards. Later, go for dinner and drinks at the **Marriott Ko Olina Beach Club** *(see p117)*.

See map on pp90–91 ←

The Best of the Rest

Tiki masks, Aloha Stadium Swap Meet

1 Aloha Stadium Swap Meet

MAP D4 ■ 99-500 Salt Lake Blvd ■ 486 6704 ■ Open 8am–3pm Wed & Sat, 6:30am–3pm Sun ■ Adm ■ www. alohastadium.hawaii.gov

The largest swap meet in the islands, this is a great place for kitsch souvenirs, alohawear, beach equipment, food trucks, and live entertainment.

2 Kō Hana Distillers

MAP C3 ■ 92-1770 Kunia Rd, Kunia ■ 649 0830 ■ Open 11am–5pm daily ■ www.kohanarum.com

Find out how the rum for your *mai tai* is made on a one-hour tour that includes tastings and a walk through the sugarcane fields.

3 Wahiawā Town

MAP C3

Primarily a military town, dusty Wahiawā, high on the central plain, is a useful stop-off for supplies when journeying through the hinterland.

4 Waikele Premium Outlets

MAP C4 ■ 94-790 Lumiana St, Waipahu, Exit 5A off H1 ■ 676 5656

This mall houses more than 50 outlet stores including Armani, Calvin Klein, and Tommy Bahama.

5 Waipahu

MAP C4

This one-time plantation town is the hub for Oʻahu's Filipino community. Activities at the large Filcom Center (94–428 Mokuola St) include dance and martial-arts classes and film screenings.

6 Tropic Lightning Museum

MAP B3 ■ 361 Waianae Ave, Schofield Barracks (request entry at Lyman Gate and bring photo ID) ■ 655 0438 ■ Open 10am–4pm Tue–Fri

Housing memorabilia from the US 25th Infantry Division (nicknamed "Tropic Lightning"), this museum helps to explain the American military history of Oʻahu.

7 Don Quijote

MAP C4 ■ 94-144 Farrington Hwy, Waipahu ■ 678 6800

Open 24 hours, this Japanese discount store makes for a convenient stop for groceries, inexpensive souvenirs, and other essentials.

8 Pearlridge Center

MAP D4 ■ 98-1005 Moanalua Rd, ʻAiea ■ 488 0981 ■ www.pearlridge online.com

This shopping mall is comprised of two main sections linked by a monorail. It is especially popular with tweens and teens.

9 ʻAiea Bowl

MAP D4 ■ 99-115 ʻAiea Heights Dr ■ 488 6854 ■ www.aieabowl.com

A family-friendly spot by day, this bustling bowling alley also has many dining options. Things liven up at night, with glow-in-the-dark "cosmic bowling" and dancing until midnight.

10 White Plains Beach

MAP B5 ■ Essex Rd & Eisenhower Rd, Kapolei

This beach has a long and soft sandy strip, mellow waves for surfers, and plenty of picnic spots for families.

Places to Eat

1 Sunnyside
MAP C3 ▪ 1017 Kilani Ave, Wahiawā ▪ 622 3663 ▪ $

This breakfast spot serves island specialties such as fried rice with hot dogs, barbequed chicken, and cream pies. Expect long lines on weekends.

2 Monkeypod Kitchen
MAP B5 ▪ 92–1048 Olani St, Kapolei ▪ 380 4086 ▪ $$

Listen to live music while enjoying farm-to-table Hawaiian food and views of the surrounding golf course.

The facade of Monkeypod Kitchen

3 Ice Garden
MAP D4 ▪ 99-115 'Aiea Heights Dr, 'Aiea Shopping Center ▪ 488 5154 ▪ $ (cash only)

Tiny, well-known spot for shave ice and home-made *mochi* (sweet Japanese rice cakes), served in flavors such as strawberry, taro, and watermelon.

4 Shiro's Saimin Haven & Family Restaurant
MAP D5 ▪ Waimalu Shopping Center, 98–020 Kamehameha Hwy, 'Aiea ▪ 488 4834 ▪ $

This shrine to Japanese-style noodle soup and plate lunches has to be seen to be believed. Founder Shiro Matsuo has lined the walls with notes expressing his philosophy of life.

5 Anna Miller's
MAP D4 ▪ 98–115 Kaonohi St, 'Aiea ▪ 487 2421 ▪ $

Come here for a choice of over 20 homemade desserts including

strawberry and lemon meringue, and pecan pies baked fresh daily.

6 Boston's North End Pizza Bakery
MAP D4 ▪ 98–302 Kamehameha Hwy, 'Aiea ▪ 487 4055 ▪ $

The pies here are Boston-style – thick edge, thin center, cheesy, saucy – and the attitude is East Coast too. That means "eat it and beat it."

7 Restaurant 604
MAP D4 ▪ 57 Arizona Memorial Dr, Honolulu ▪ 888 7616 ▪ $$

Live music and great views feature at this friendly, open-air marina-side pub. Try the Kalua pork nachos.

8 Roy's Ko Olina
MAP B5 ▪ 92–1220 Aliinui Dr, Ko Olina Golf Club ▪ 676 7697 ▪ $$

Award-winning restaurateur and chef Roy Yamaguchi perfects his Hawaii fusion cuisine, while bringing the excitement of his open-plan kitchen to the islands.

9 Ichiriki
MAP D4 ▪ 98–150 Kaonohi St, 'Aiea ▪ 484 2222 ▪ $$

At this restaurant specializing in savory *nabe* (Japanese hot pot), you get to choose the broth, vegetables, seafood, meat, and noodles. Then you cook it yourself.

10 'Ama 'Ama
MAP B5 ▪ Aulani Resort, 92–1185 Ali'inui Dr, Ko Olina ▪ 674 6200 ▪ $$$

Disney's most lauded restaurant serves modern interpretations of classic Hawaiian dishes in a scenic beachfront setting.

See map on pp90–91 ←

TOP 10 Windward Oʻahu

Going from Kailua to Kahuku means traveling from town to country. Kailua, a commuter town of Honolulu, is an upscale neighborhood of beach and lake homes, while Kāneʻohe accommodates a Marine base and Hawaiian homesteads. North from Kāneʻohe, the route along Kamehameha Highway passes a string of sandy beaches and brooding valleys, watched over by the Koʻolau Mountain Range.

Kayaking to the Ahu o Laka Sandbar

1 Ahu o Laka Sandbar
MAP E3

At low tide on a weekend, drive slowly on Kamehameha Highway just past Heʻeia Kea Boat Harbor. A little way offshore, you'll see watercraft of every description clustered around seemingly nothing at all. In fact, just above sea level is a sandbar, and locals like to gather here, light the hibachi and hang out.

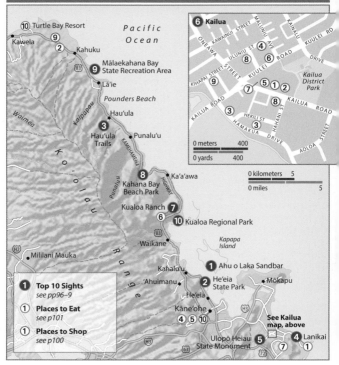

WINDWARD OʻAHU

Turtle Bay Resort
Kawela
Kahuku
Mālaekahana Bay State Recreation Area
Lāʻie
Pounders Beach
Hauʻula
Hauʻula Trails
Punaluʻu
Kahana Bay Beach Park
Kaʻaʻawa
Kualoa Ranch
Kualoa Regional Park
Waikane
Mililani Mauka
Kahaluʻu
ʻAhuimanu
Heʻeia
Kāneʻohe
Ahu o Laka Sandbar
Heʻeia State Park
Mōkapu
Kapapa Island
Ulopō Heiau State Monument
Lanikai

Pacific Ocean

Kailua
ONEAWA STREET
KAWAINUI STREET
MALUNIU AVE
KAHALU
ULUNIU AVE
KUULEI RD
KIHAPAI STREET
KUULEI ROAD
Kailua District Park
KAILUA ROAD
KAILUA ROAD
HEKILI ST
HAMAKUA DRIVE
AOLOA STREET

| 0 meters | 400 |
| 0 yards | 400 |

| 0 kilometers | 5 |
| 0 miles | 5 |

See Kailua map, above

1 Top 10 Sights
see pp96–9

1 Places to Eat
see p101

1 Places to Shop
see p100

② Heʻeia State Park and Fishponds

Surrounded by mangrove swamp, this grassy, well-maintained state park *(see p31)* is located on Kāneʻohe Bay, which contains Oʻahu's only barrier reef. The park offers a view of the long Heʻeia fishpond, the largest intact aquaculture zone in the islands. There are several other fishponds in the vicinity. When in use, fingerlings of the prized *ʻamaʻama* (mullet) and *ʻahole* (Hawaiian flagtail) swim into the rock-walled ponds through vertical gates called *mākaha*, but are unable to swim out. In this way, the fish are successfully farmed.

③ Hauʻula Trails

MAP D2 ■ **From Kamehameha (Hwy 83), the trails are reached by Hauʻula Homestead Rd and Maʻakua Rd**

Hauʻula ("red *hau* tree" in Hawaiian) is the starting point for three very good rambles that range from easy to moderate (a fourth hike, Sacred Falls, is closed indefinitely due to landslide danger). The two most worthwhile treks are Maʻakua Loop and Maʻakua Ridge (aka Papali Trail); both offer good views, interesting plants, and guavas in their late summer and fall season.

④ Lanikai

MAP F4

Developed as a beach retreat in the 1920s, beautiful Lanikai (which is

reached by a beach road south of Kailua) remains one of the most sought-after addresses on the island of Oʻahu. This tight-knit neighborhood hosts community plays and an exceptional pre-Christmas craft fair.

Ancient temple at Ulupō Heiau

⑤ Ulupō Heiau State Monument

MAP E4

Some locals still visit this historic location to arrange leaf-wrapped gift bundles on the massive rock platform, formerly a site of prayer, sacrifice, ceremony, and divination. Likely built during the time of Kamehameha I, the *heiau* continued in use until the ancient religion was officially abandoned. To find it, head toward Kailua on Highway 61, turn left into Uluʻoa Street at the Windward YMCA, park in the Y lot or along the street and follow the signs.

Sun-worshipers relaxing on beautiful Lanikai beach

6 Kailua
MAP F4

This country-chic town consists of a few blocks of shops and restaurants, peaceful 1960s-era neighborhoods, and a string of popular beaches *(see p49)*. Park along Kailua Road and explore on foot, weaving in and out of interesting gift and clothing shops. At No. 600, Lanikai Juice serves delicious smoothies and juices.

Open-air shopping mall at Kailua

7 Kualoa Ranch
MAP E3 ■ Kualoa Ranch 49–560 Kamehameha Hwy ■ 237 7321 ■ www.kualoa.com

The valley and rolling hillsides of Kualoa were once a sacred place of refuge, then passed to missionary descendants from royal hands. Today, Kualoa is a working cattle ranch, as well as a park where visitors can enjoy equestrian experiences and movie tours *(see p47)*. The ranch is a popular filming spot, appearing in movies and TV shows such as *Jurassic Park* and *Lost*.

Cattle on the green pastures of Kualoa Ranch

SHRIMP TRUCKS

Northbound on Kamehameha Highway between Kāne'ohe and Kahuku, you'll encounter a string of shrimp trucks, some in food trucks, others in roadside stands. It all began with a single shrimp aquaculture operation, which sparked a North Shore love affair with crustaceans. Stop at Romy's Kahuku Prawns and Shrimp *(56-781 Kamehameha Hwy, Kahuku)* for fresh shrimp cooked with butter and garlic.

8 Kahana Bay Beach Park/Kahana Valley
MAP D2 ■ 52-222 Kamehameha Hwy ■ 587 0300

State-owned watershed land, the deep Kahana Valley is fronted by an 8-acre (3-ha) city and county park. The park has a sandy beach, bathrooms, picnic tables, a large number of chickens (escaped fowl are ubiquitous all along this coast), and the remnants of two fishponds. Watch for fishers wading out to catch *akule* (big-eyed scad).

9 Mālaekahana Bay State Recreation Area
MAP D1

This curving sandy beach is distinguished by bare-bones beach homes available for rent, a reef that keeps the inshore waters calm, and Goat Island, a wild and beautiful bird sanctuary. Mālaekahana Bay is also home to two camping areas, with full facilities, including restrooms, outdoor showers, picnic tables, and drinking water.

Mokoliʻi Island seen from Kualoa Park

10 Kualoa Regional Park
MAP E3

The flat, windy Kualoa Regional Park features a narrow sandy beach and shallow inshore ponds. It is a fantastic spot for activities such as kite-flying, snorkeling, launching watercraft, picnicking, and camping (by permit). The clearly visible triangle-shaped peak sitting on the ocean is the island of Mokoliʻi (see p30), popular with kayakers.

A DAY ON THE WINDWARD COAST

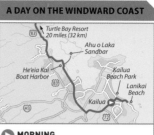

▶ **MORNING**

Begin your itinerary by heading straight for **Kailua**, where you can stop off at **Agnes' Portuguese Bake Shop** food truck (5 Hoʻolai St) for coffee and *malasadas* (Portuguese doughnuts, freshly made and eaten hot).

Treat yourself to Hawaiian scents and lotions at **Lanikai Bath and Body** (600 Kailua Rd). If you're feeling peckish, try an authentic plate lunch at **Fatboy's** (301A Hahani St) for a true taste of the island.

Then head for **Kailua Beach Park** (see p49) or **Lanikai Beach** (see p49) for the afternoon. Either is good for surfing, swimming, snorkeling, and boating.

AFTERNOON

You could opt for a sun-soaked lazy afternoon, but if you fancy a little more activity, rent some form of watercraft from Sun and Salt Adventures Hawaii (www.sunandsalthawaii.com) or from Kailua Beach Adventures (www.kailuabeachadventures.com). Then, either paddle out to the Nā Mokulua islets (see p49) off Kailua Beach or steer over to **Heʻeia Kai Boat Harbor** and head to the **Ahu o Laka Sandbar** (see p96).

If you do plan to spend more time on the coast, consider reserving one of the luxurious rooms at the **Turtle Bay Resort** (see pp116–17). You can loiter your way from Kailua to Kahuku, leaving mid-afternoon and making one or two stops, and still arrive by check-in time. You won't have to face the long drive back across the island, and you can dine in the extra-ordinary **Alaia** restaurant (p101).

See map on p96 ←

Places to Shop

1 Under a Hula Moon
MAP F4 ▪ 600 Kailua Rd, Kailua Shopping Center ▪ 261 4252

A delightful, Hawaiian-themed gift shop, Under a Hula Moon sells clothes, home accessories, jewelry, and artworks.

2 Bookends in Kailua
MAP F4 ▪ 600 Kailua Rd, Kailua Shopping Center ▪ 261 1996

This bookstore is run by readers for readers and has comfy chairs and a mix of new and used books, stacked high. It has a good children's section.

3 Foodland
MAP F4 ▪ 108 Hekili St, Kailua ▪ 261 3211

The area's largest supermarket stocks almost everything – from snacks and health supplies to local produce such as macadamia nuts.

4 Manoa Chocolate Hawaii
MAP F4 ▪ 333 Uluniu St, Kailua ▪ 263 6292

Most of the ingredients in the chocolate bars at this small shop and factory are sourced in Hawaii. They also offer tasting tours.

5 Aesthetic Hawaii Gallery
MAP F4 ▪ 602 Kailua Rd, Kailua Shopping Center ▪ 548 0901

Kailua Koa wood craft, *lauhala* (woven pandanus) creations, and ceramics are among the treasures for sale here. They are mostly made by local artists.

Inside the Aesthetic Hawaii Gallery

6 Kailua General Store
MAP F4 ▪ 316 Kuulei Rd, Kailua ▪ 261 5740

Island artworks, local honey, clothes, natural soaps, handmade gift items, and refreshing shave ice can be found at this friendly concept store.

7 Red Bamboo
MAP F4 ▪ 602 Kailua Rd, Kailua ▪ 263 3174

Pineapple, shell, and tropical flower prints embellish the many home decor and gift items at this merry shop. Locally made jewelry, paintings, and other fine art are also on offer.

8 Coco's Trading Post
MAP F4 ▪ 539 Kailua Rd, Kailua ▪ 892 5642

Browse the eclectic collection of Hawaiian-made and recycled gifts and souvenirs at this popular spot.

9 Only Show in Town
MAP D1 ▪ 56–901 Kamehameha Hwy, Kahuku ▪ 293 1295

Antiques and collectibles from all eras in Hawaiian history, as well as from a beguiling miscellany of other times and places, are available here.

10 Kanileʻa Ukulele
MAP E4 ▪ 46–56 Kamehameha Hwy, Kāneʻohe ▪ 234 2868 ▪ Factory tours: 9:30am Mon–Fri

This is one of the best places to purchase an authentic, locally made ukulele. Lessons are available, too.

Places to Eat

PRICE CATEGORIES
Price categories include a three-course meal for one, a glass of house wine, and all unavoidable extra charges including tax.

$ under $30 $$ $30–$60 $$$ over $60

1 Buzz's Original Steak House
MAP F4 ▪ 413 Kawailoa Rd, Lanikai ▪ 261 4661 ▪ $$

This venerable spot – a warren of dim rooms scented with the delicious aroma of grilling meat – serves surf and turf to a broad clientele from Lanikai millionaires to sandy surfers.

2 Kahaku Farm Café
MAP C1 ▪ 56–800 Kamehameha Hwy, Kahuku ▪ 628 0639 ▪ $

Most of the vegetarian items here are made with freshly picked fruit and vegetables from the 5-acre (2-ha) family farm. Try the banana bread and the Tropi-kale smoothie.

3 Nalu Health Bar & Café
MAP F4 ▪ 131 Hekili St, Kailua ▪ 263 6258 ▪ $

Choose from a wide variety of fresh-pressed juices, tropical smoothies, organic açai bowls, fresh salads, and loaded wraps – all made with locally sourced fresh ingredients.

4 Haleiwa Joe's
MAP E4 ▪ 46–336 Haʻikū Rd, Kāneʻohe ▪ 247 6671 ▪ $$

Call to check Joe's isn't reserved for a wedding – neighboring Haʻikū Gardens does a booming bride-and-groom business. If open, expect steaks, seafood, and sandwiches.

5 Adela's Country Eatery
MAP E4 ▪ 45–1151 Kamehameha Hwy ▪ 236 2366 ▪ $

This family-owned takeout spot is known for its colorful handmade pasta, which is created using locally grown breadfruit, taro, avocado, and sweet potato.

6 Aunty Pat's Café
MAP E3 ▪ Kualoa Ranch, 49–560 Kamehameha Hwy ▪ 237 7321 ▪ $$

Named for a descendant of the Kualoa Ranch's founder, this casual café serves breakfasts and lunches, including gourmet burgers made fresh from the ranch's herd.

Burger and fries – a popular meal

7 Boots & Kimo's Homestyle Kitchen
MAP F4 ▪ 1020 Keolu Dr, Kailua ▪ 263 7929 ▪ $

Popular with locals and tourists, this welcoming café often has lengthy lines for its delicious banana macadamia nut pancakes.

8 Uahi Island Grill
MAP F4 ▪ 33 Aulike St, Kailua ▪ 266 4646 ▪ $

This casual local institution serves contemporary island favorites as well as traditional plate lunches.

9 The Boardroom
MAP F4 ▪ 44 Kainehe St, Kailua ▪ 807 5640 ▪ $$

Cozy tapas lounge with modern, surfer vibes. Items on the dinner and drinks menu are all locally sourced – the ahi tuna tartare is a must try.

10 Alaia
MAP C1 ▪ 57–091 Kamehameha Hwy, Turtle Bay Resort ▪ 293 6020 ▪ $$$

With ingredients sourced from the resort's own Kuilima Farm, Alaia offers truly local, seasonal Hawaiian specialties.

See map on p96 ←

TOP 10 South Shore

It's an easy drive around the South Shore of Oʻahu from Waikīkī to the rural village of Waimānalo, but over those 12 miles (19 km), you experience the island's multidimensional nature. After the exclusive community of Kāhala, you come to a series of densely populated valley neighborhoods. Each of these climbs from a coral-fringed beach to the apex of a deep valley in the classic Hawaiian land division known as an *ahupuaʻa*. At the island's edge, the coast provides an ecologically fragile landscape, before giving way to mile upon mile of golden sand, bordering the island's ranch lands.

Admiring the view from a rocky outcrop at Makapuʻu Beach Park

SOUTH SHORE

1. **Top 10 Sights**
   see pp102–5
1. **Places to Eat**
   see p107
1. **Places to Shop**
   see p106

1 Makapuʻu Beach Park
MAP F5

This park (see p50) contains some of Oʻahu's most beloved landmarks – the beach (a bodysurfer's hub), the nearby lighthouse, and the shore trail. Just over the rocks lies "baby beach," where shallow tide pools are safe for young children to splash around in. Manana, better known as Rabbit Island, is a dramatic landmark standing offshore.

2 Eternity Beach
MAP F5

This gorgeous little pocket of beach, also known as Halona Cove, has appeared in many Hollywood films, such as the 1950s movie *From Here to Eternity* and the *Jurassic World* series. It's also a popular fishing spot but not ideal for swimming due to the powerful waves. To find this gem, follow the sandy trail down from the Halona Blowhole Lookout parking lot.

3 Kuliʻouʻou Beach Park
MAP F6

This family-friendly beach park on Maunalua Bay offers a number of picnic sites, scenic views, and, at low tide, the opportunity for novice kayakers to take to the water. To get there, from Kalanianaʻole, turn right onto Kuliʻouʻou Road, left onto Summer Street and right again onto Bay Street, which shortly comes to a dead end in the parking lot.

Small, idyllic beach at Hanauma Bay

4 Hanauma Bay
MAP F6

Keyhole-shaped Hanauma Bay, with its bright-blue waters and soft white sand, is one of the most spectacular sights in the islands, and highly recommended for swimming and snorkeling. It's a good idea to go early in the day as both visitor numbers and parking spaces are limited (see p42).

5 Paikō Lagoon State Reserve
MAP F5

The Paikō Peninsula (its name derives from a Portuguese former resident called Pico) offers birdwatching, fishing, snorkeling, and relative seclusion. From Kalanianaʻole, turn right onto narrow Paikō Drive, park on the street and take the beach access trail to the water. Turn left (east) and find your spot past the second to last house. Bring food and water with you, as there are no services at the reserve.

Canoes at Kuliʻouʻou Beach Park

The breathtaking landscape surrounding Kāhala Beach

6 Kāhala Beach
MAP E6

This remote stretch of golden sand, hidden by suburban Kāhala's ritzy homes, offers snorkeling, reef-fishing, and sunbathing. To get here from Waikīkī, take Diamond Head Road until it becomes Kāhala Avenue. In the 4,400 to 4,800 blocks of Kāhala Avenue, watch out for several narrow paths, marked by blue beach access signs (park on the street). The bigger stretch of Waiʻalae Beach Park is just beyond Kapakahi Stream bridge.

On a canoe in Maunalua Bay

7 Maunalua Bay Beach Park
MAP F6

This sun-baked park has picnic tables, restrooms, and some grassy areas for play. It's a launching point for excursions onto Maunalua Bay, from outrigger canoe paddling and water-skiing to fishing, diving, and snorkeling trips.

8 Bellows Field Beach Park
MAP F4 ■ Camping by permit only

Although located on a military installation (which includes an army reserve camp where Marines practice amphibious landings), this sprawling beach and campsite with ample parking is a public facility on weekends and holidays. Many consider it the best of the Waimānalo beaches; it's great for bodyboarding, boogie-boarding, and surfing (see p48).

9 Sandy Beach
MAP F5

Renowned for the constant winds that make kite-flying a feature and for the surf that breaks very near to its shore, Sandy Beach is very popular with bodyboarders and surfers. Great caution should be taken as the waves routinely slam unsuspecting waders into

KITE FLYING

On any suitably windy day at Sandy Beach, the sky is bright with colorful kites. Flyers from the ages of 6 to 60 play out the lines, straining against the wind. Traditionally, Hawaiian kites were made from hau wood, covered with kappa or woven lauhala, with olonā cord used for the string. Skill was needed both to make and fly them.

the rock-hard sand. Don't turn
your back on the ocean – here,
or anywhere else *(see p51)*.

10 Waimānalo Bay State Recreation Area

MAP F5

Here you catch sight of uninterrupted
white sand that stretches 3 miles
(5 km) along the coast. The facility
includes Waimānalo Beach Park also
known as Hūnānāniho, to the south,
and the recreation area to the north.
Both offer prime picnic areas, campsites, restrooms, and showers. The
park is on the road but the recreation
area is secluded in an ironwood
grove. Car parking is free but you'll
need a permit for camping.

Lifeguard hut at Waimānalo Beach

SOUTH SHORE TOUR

▶ MORNING

A South Shore circular driving
tour makes for a great all-day
itinerary. Starting from **Waikīkī**,
pick up breakfast pastries from
Fendu Boulangerie in **Manoa
Marketplace** *(2752 Woodlawn Dr)*.

Head back down south, take the
H1 east, and finish off the morning
with a water adventure, such
as water-skiing or diving, at
Maunalua Bay. Reserve ahead at
water activity shops at Hawaii Kai
Towne Center or Koko Marina
Center. For a more sedate pursuit,
take binoculars and go birdwatching on the edge of the **Paikō
Lagoon State Reserve** *(see p103)*.

Back on Kalaniana'ole, grab
a quick lunch at **Kona Brewing
Co.** *(see p107)* or any one of a
dozen inexpensive restaurants at
Koko Marina Center *(see p106)*.

AFTERNOON

Cruise slowly around the island's
edge, stopping to view the **Hālona
Blow Hole** *(see p43)* and watch
the bodysurfers and kite-fliers at
Sandy Beach. November through
May the Blow Hole is a vantage
point to see whales migrating.

At **Makapu'u Wayside**, park
and make the easy hour-long,
2-mile (3-km) trek up and down
the old lighthouse road *(see
p46)*; the views will stay with
you for a long time.

Afterwards, stop for a drink or
a bite to eat at the **Hawaiian
Island Café** *(seep107)* and enjoy
a refreshing swim at **Waimānalo
Beach** before heading home via
⬤ the Pali Highway.

See map on p102 ←

Places to Shop

Browsing inside Whole Foods Market

They sell fresh *kahuku* corn, fruits, chilled coconuts, tropical flowers, fresh or dried fish, and specialties such as *pasteles* (Puerto Rican tamales) and *poke* (raw fish and seaweed salad).

① Whole Foods Market
MAP E6 ▪ Kāhala Mall, 4211 Waiʻalae Ave ▪ 738 0820

This widely popular chain is a one-stop store for an array of locally produced, natural and organic food, and gift items. It stocks an extensive range of bakery products, cheeses, beer and wine, and pre-packed to go meals including sushi and pizza.

② 33 Butterflies
MAP E6 ▪ Kahala Mall, 4211 Waiʻalae Ave ▪ 380 8585

Locally owned boutique selling women's wear in chic, island styles.

③ T&C Surf
MAP E6 ▪ Kāhala Mall, 4211 Waiʻalae Ave ▪ 733 5699

Since the 1970s, this shop has been selling quality surfing and skateboarding gear and apparel.

④ Paperie
MAP E6 ▪ Kāhala Mall, 4211 Waiʻalae Ave ▪ 735 6464

The Paperie offers fine- quality paper goods such as Hawaii-themed cards, stationery, and wedding supplies.

⑤ Roadside Stands
MAP F5

Keep an eye out for charming roadside stands near Waimānalo.

⑥ Koko Marina Center
MAP F6 ▪ 7192 Kalanianaʻole Hwy ▪ 395 4737

This shopping center includes a vast supermarket, theater complex, many restaurants, and places to rent water gear or arrange excursions along the coast.

⑦ The Compleat Kitchen
MAP E6 ▪ Kāhala Mall, 4211 Waiʻalae Ave ▪ 737 5827

Honolulu's first upscale kitchen supply store stocks gorgeous bamboo cutting boards and other high-quality gifts for foodies.

⑧ ʻAina Haina Shopping Center
MAP E5 ▪ 820–850 W. Hind Dr, Honolulu ▪ 732 7736

Anchored by the local grocery chain Foodland Farms, this modern strip mall is great for local goodies including Hawaii's special apple bananas and fresh tuna *poke*.

⑨ Sugarcane Shop
MAP E6 ▪ 1137 11th Ave ▪ 739 2263

Colorful and quaint gift shop for local, handmade products such as soaps, beach bags, books, and puzzles, as well as vintage treasures.

⑩ Hawaii Kai Towne Center and Hawaii Kai Shopping Center
MAP F5 ▪ Towne Center: 333 Keahole St; 396 0766 ▪ Shopping Center: 377 Keahole St; 396 4402

These side-by-side open malls feature a wealth of options such as grocery shops, dive shops, boat charter firms, and restaurants, as well as banks and dry-cleaners.

See map on p102

Places to Eat

PRICE CATEGORIES

Price categories include a three-course meal for one, a glass of house wine, and all unavoidable extra charges including tax.

$ under $30 **$$** $30–$60 **$$$** over $60

1 Island Brew Coffeehouse
MAP F5 ▪ 377 Keahole St, Honolulu ▪ 394 8770 ▪ $

Healthy sandwich bagels, açai bowls, and 100 percent Hawaiian coffee are served at this simple breakfast and lunch spot. There is a beautiful view over the water from the back patio.

2 The Counter
MAP E6 ▪ Kāhala Mall, 4211 Wai'alae Ave ▪ 739 5100 ▪ $

You can build your own burger here, or try one of the signature offerings: the Counter Burger is stacked high with cheese, fried onion strings, mushrooms, salad, and garlic aioli.

3 Olive Tree Café
MAP E6 ▪ 4614 Kīlauea Ave, Kaimuki ▪ 737 0303 ▪ $$

One of the few Mediterranean restaurants in the islands, this spot routinely wins awards for its great Greek fare (cash and takeout only).

4 Hawaiian Island Café
MAP F5 ▪ 41–1537 Kalaniana'ole Hwy, Waimanalo ▪ 312 4006 ▪ $

This cozy spot specializes in huge sandwiches, pizzas, and fresh juices, all made with organic ingredients.

5 Zippy's
MAP E6 ▪ 4134 Wai'alae Ave, Kāhala ▪ 733 3730 ▪ $

This South Shore outpost of one of the island's most popular chains serves inexpensive, island-style comfort food such as chicken *katsu* and *saimin* noodle soup and house signature chili.

6 Roy's Restaurant
MAP F5 ▪ 6600 Kalaniana'ole Hwy, Hawaii Kai ▪ 396 7697 ▪ $$$

The flagship of the sprawling Roy's Restaurant empire continues to deliver its trademarks: high-energy atmosphere, a dramatic open-plan kitchen, and a menu that ranges from salsa to Szechuan (see p61).

7 Koko Head Café
MAP C7 ▪ 1120 12th Ave, Honolulu ▪ 732 8920 ▪ $

Locals head to this brunch diner for a Pan-Asian twist on breakfast classics. Expect a line and take some kimchi bacon cheddar scones home (see p60).

8 Jack's Restaurant
MAP E5 ▪ 'Aina Haina Shopping Center, 820 W. Hind ▪ 373 4034 ▪ $

Stop by this neighborhood spot to discover Jack's giant Special Biscuits and omelets with kimchee fried rice. Breakfast is served until 2pm.

10 Pipeline Bakeshop & Creamery
MAP F6 ▪ 3632 Wai'alae Ave ▪ 738 8200 ▪ $

There's no shortage of freshly baked, hot *malasadas* (doughnuts) in O'ahu, but this small bakery makes some of the best.

9 Kona Brewing Co.
MAP F6 ▪ Koko Marina Center, 7192 Kalaniana'ole Hwy ▪ 396 5662 ▪ $

The first O'ahu brewpub by Big Island-based Kona Brewing, located on the docks of Koko Marina, serves burgers, salads, casual fare, and, of course, beer.

Entrance of Kona Brewing Co.

Streetsmart

Brightly colored surfboards in front of the ocean

Getting Around

Arriving by Air

Hawaii is one of the most isolated archipelagos in the world, so it's no surprise that most travelers arrive on O'ahu by air. **Honolulu International Airport (HNL)**, located 9 miles (14 km) northwest of Waikīkī, is one of the busiest airports in the US. Most major domestic and international airlines fly to HNL, including **American Airlines**, **Alaska Airlines**, **Air New Zealand**, **Air Canada**, **Qantas** and **WestJet**.

The complimentary Wiki-Wiki Bus shuttles between HNL's three terminals and the gates. Information booths can be found in the Baggage Claim area and outside the Foreign Arrivals area.

After the Baggage Claim area, there will be shuttles and taxis (look for the yellow Taxi Dispatcher for service) to take you to your hotel. A one-way taxi trip to Waikīkī costs about $45. Shuttles cost about $18 per passenger to Waikīkī.

Several car rental companies have registration counters in the Baggage Claim area. Additional car-rental companies have off-site lots, and their vans are waiting outside on ground level to pick passengers up. If you are traveling really light (your baggage must fit under the seat), **TheBus** is the cheapest option, at $3 for a one-way fare to Waikīkī. Take either the No. 19 or No. 20 bus.

Arriving by Sea

Numerous cruise lines have O'ahu on their itinerary, arriving mostly during the winter months. They dock at either of the two cruise-ship terminals on Honolulu Harbor – Pier 2 and Pier 11, by the Aloha Tower. Both are in downtown Honolulu and about 3 miles (5 km) from Waikīkī. Taxis and shuttles can take you from here to your hotel, and there's a car-rental company just a few blocks south of the piers, on Ala Moana Blvd.

Driving

Unless you're planning to stick to the Honolulu and Waikīkī area, it may be wise to rent a car so that you can see more of the island. Virtually every major national car-rental company is represented in Honolulu, such as **Avis**, **Enterprise**, and **National**. Car-rental companies in Waikīkī will often have better rates.

Seat belts for everyone and approved car seats for children under four are mandatory. Pedestrians always have the right of way. Do not use your cell phone while driving, or you'll face a hefty fine. Keep the gas tank at least half-full – distances between gas stations may be long. Gas prices are much higher in Hawaii than on the US mainland.

Honolulu has its traffic challenges, especially when commuters come in and go out of town, but outside the city, driving is more relaxed. Locals will rarely sound their car horns – it's considered rude to do so unless in an emergency – so check your rear-view mirror often to see if someone wants to pass you.

In Hawaii directions aren't given in terms of east, west, north, and south. Instead, you will often hear the words 'Ewa (toward 'Ewa Beach), *mauka* (toward the mountains), and *makai* (toward the ocean).

Buses

You can get just about anywhere on O'ahu by **TheBus**, the island's public transportation system. You can purchase a one-way fare, either paid by cash in exact change or by a reloadable Holo Card, or a 1-day or monthly pass; the 1-day pass allows for unlimited rides. Both the passes and Holo Cards are sold at **7-Eleven** stores and various other outlets and supermarkets. Convenience stores in Honolulu stock the bus map, which also has a handy guide to Honolulu's many attractions.

Trains

A brand-new urban rail rapid transit system known as the Honolulu Rail Transit, the first of its kind in Hawaii, is set to open in late 2023. The first phase of this ambitious project will link East Kapolei to the Aloha Stadium. The second

phase, scheduled for completion in 2031, will continue the line to the Ala Moana Center in Honolulu.

Trolleys

The open-air trolleys you'll see rolling around town, run by **Waikiki Trolley**, are a fun and cheap way to get around. There are four routes in total: the red line covers Chinatown and the historic sites; the blue line covers Diamond Head and ocean viewpoints; the green line covers some of the island's favorite restaurants; and the pink line covers shopping destinations. Tickets can be purchased on board, at tour desks, or through the website.

Taxis

For short, in-town trips you can get a taxi in front of any major hotel, and restaurants are happy to call a taxi for you after your meal. Many hotels also provide a shuttle service, usually to shopping destinations and sometimes also to sights. Both taxis and shuttles are called in advance rather than hailed on the street. Rates are fixed, but pre-reserved round trips can often be much more economical.

Ride-sharing firms such as **Uber** and **Lyft** operate in Oʻahu, mostly in Honolulu. Other good taxi companies include **Charley's Taxi**, **Roberts Hawaii Express Shuttle**, **Yellow Cab Honolulu Taxi**, and **Hawaii23 Shuttle**.

Cycling

Despite some dedicated bike lanes, Oʻahu is not a bike-friendly island yet, though the city of Honolulu has plans to improve this in the future. Several outfitters offer downhill and mountain biking tours, such as **Bike Hawaii**. If you do decide to go out on your own, useful bike route maps are available from the **Hawaii Department of Transportation**.

Walking

Many areas of Honolulu are easily navigable on foot, including laid-back Waikīkī, historic Chinatown, and up-and-coming Kakaʻako; the city is also home to several parks that are perfect for a wander. In addition, a number of hiking trails can be found close to the city, including the spectacular trail that leads to the top of the Diamond Head crater.

Outside of the city, there are even more excellent hiking opportunities available, thanks to the countless trails scattered around the island. Note, however, that many of these trails require 4WD transport to reach them.

DIRECTORY

ARRIVING BY AIR

Air Canada
w aircanada.com

Air New Zealand
w airnewzealand.com

Alaska Airlines
w alaskaair.com

American Airlines
w aa.com

Honolulu International Airport (HNL)
w airports.hawaii.gov/hnl

Qantas
w qantas.com

WestJet
w westjet.com

DRIVING

Avis
w avis.com

Enterprise
w enterprise.com

National
w nationalcar.com

BUSES

7-Eleven
w 7elevenhawaii.com

TheBus
w thebus.org

TROLLEYS

Waikiki Trolley
w waikikitrolley.com

TAXIS

Charley's Taxi
w charleystaxi.com

Hawaii23 Shuttle
w hawaii23.com

Lyft
w lyft.com

Roberts Hawaii Express Shuttle
w robertshawaii.com

Uber
w uber.com

Yellow Cab Honolulu Taxi
w honolulu-taxi.com

CYCLING

Bike Hawaii
w bikehawaii.com

Hawaii Department of Transportation
w hidot.hawaii.gov

Practical Information

Passports and Visas

For entry requirements, including visas, consult your nearest US embassy or check the **US State Department**'s website.

Visitors from most European countries, including the UK, and from Australia, New Zealand, Chile, Japan, Singapore, and South Korea need a passport that is valid for at least six months from the date that they plan to enter Oʻahu. They must also apply online for an **ESTA** (Electronic System for Travel Authorization) in advance of traveling to Hawaii. Canadians must show a valid passport. Other foreign nationals need a valid passport and a tourist visa, obtainable from a US consulate or embassy in their home country. Having proof of a return ticket is also strongly recommended.

Customs Information

You can find information on the laws relating to goods and currency taken in or out of Hawaii on the **Go Hawaii** official tourist board website.

Most meat, vegetables, fruit, and plants cannot be brought into Oʻahu. This is meant to protect the island's unique environment, which is rather fragile due to its isolated geographical location. Any luggage leaving Oʻahu is subject to an agricultural search, since only certain fruits and flowers may be taken out, such as pine-apples and *lei*, so make sure you ask about this when you're purchasing such items.

Never take any natural objects – such as coral, sand, and lava rocks – home with you from Hawaii. Not only can this cause damage to local ecosystems, it is also illegal in most cases and offensive to many Hawaiians who believe that everything – every stone, every shell, every plant – on Hawaii is connected, and has both a life and a place of its own. Known as Pele's Curse, taking lava rocks off the islands is especially *kapu* (forbidden) and is believed to bring bad luck.

Government Advice

Now more than ever, it is important to consult both your and the US government's advice before traveling. The **UK Foreign, Commonwealth & Development Office (FCDO)**, the US State Department, the **Australian Department of Foreign Affairs and Trade**, and the State of Hawaii's **Safe Travels** website offer the latest information on security, health, and local regulations.

Insurance

We recommend that you take out a comprehensive insurance policy covering theft, loss of belongings, medical care, cancellations and delays, and read the small print carefully. If adventure activities or water sports are part of your itinerary, check that these are covered by your insurance provider.

Insurance is particularly important when traveling in Oʻahu as the cost of medical care is high everywhere in the US. If you have a mainland health insurance plan, you should check to see if it is accepted in Hawaii.

Health

Hawaii, including Oʻahu, has a world-class health-care system. Payment of medical expenses is the patient's responsibility. It is therefore important to arrange comprehensive medical insurance before you travel.

There are several major medical centers in the city of Honolulu, including **Queen's Medical Center**, **Kaiser Permanente**, **Straub Medical Center**, and the **Kapiʻolani Medical Center**. There are clinics all over the island, too, and most resort hotels have doctors on call. Longs Drugs and Walgreens are good general pharmacies for prescriptions and over-the-counter medicines.

Tap water in Oʻahu is perfectly safe to drink, but do not drink from or swim in streams, ponds, rivers, waterfalls, or freshwater pools since you may run the risk of getting infected with leptospirosis, a bacterial disease that can be fatal if not treated in time.

For information regarding COVID-19 vaccination requirements, consult government advice.

Remember to protect yourself from Hawaii's powerful rays by wearing

a hat, sunglasses, and reef-safe sunblock. Avoid being out in high temperatures for long periods, and drink plenty of fluids.

Be careful when swimming in the ocean – many beaches can be safe in summer but are pounded by dangerous surf in winter. The **Hawaii Beach Safety** website provides up-to-date information on surf and wind conditions. Lifeguards are stationed at the most popular beaches. Be wary of using unguarded beaches, especially if you aren't used to identifying dangerous currents.

Watch out for scorpions in the arid regions, and for centipedes and mosquitoes in the rainforests. Out in the water, the box jellyfish and Portuguese man-of-war can deliver painful stings, while coral and sea urchins can be quite sharp if accidentally stepped on, and can also cause infections in any resulting cuts that aren't cleaned properly.

Smoking, Alcohol and Drugs

Smoking, including e-cigarettes, is prohibited in all public spaces, such as shops, restaurants, and bars. The minimum age to both drink and purchase tobacco products is 21. It is illegal to drink in a public park, including beaches, and to carry an open container of alcohol in your vehicle. Recreational use of cannabis is illegal.

ID

Visitors to O'ahu should carry ID with them at all times. Besides requiring ID for entry into Hawaii, you will need it as proof of age to purchase alcohol and cigarettes, and for vehicle, watersport, and bicycle rentals.

Personal Security

Hawaii is generally remarkably safe, and violent crime is rare. However, theft can be a problem, and tourists' rental cars are often targeted. Always lock your car, even if you are leaving it for just a few moments. Never leave anything of value in view. Remember to make use of the safe in your hotel (or the lock boxes in rental properties) to store your jewelry, cash, and other valuables. If you have anything stolen, report the crime within 24 hours to the nearest police station and take ID with you. Get a copy of the crime report to make an insurance claim.

While crime in Honolulu is not nearly the problem it is in some of the other major US cities, Hawaii's capital city has its share of less salubrious neighborhoods. Check with your hotel concierge about areas to avoid, especially late at night.

As in the rest of the US, dialing 911 in O'ahu will put you in touch with the **Emergency Services**.

As a rule, Hawaiians are very accepting of all people, regardless of their race, gender, or sexuality. Hawaii was the first US state to consider legalizing same-sex marriage, a ruling that became official in 2013. If you do feel unsafe, the **Safe Space Alliance** pinpoints your nearest place of refuge.

Honolulu, especially Waikīkī, has LGBTQ+-friendly accommodations, restaurants, and bars. Queen's Surf Beach is popular with the local LGBTQ+ community.

DIRECTORY

PASSPORTS AND VISAS
ESTA
w esta.cbp.dhs.gov

US State Department
w travel.state.gov

CUSTOMS INFORMATION
Go Hawaii
w gohawaii.com

GOVERNMENT ADVICE
Australian Department of Foreign Affairs and Trade
w smartraveller.gov.au

Safe Travels
w travel.hawaii.gov

UK Foreign, Commonwealth & Development Office (FCDO)
w gov.uk/foreign-travel-advice

HEALTH
Kaiser Permanente
w kpinhawaii.org

Kapi'olani Medical Center
w hawaiipacifichealth.org

Hawaii Beach Safety
w hawaiibeachsafety.com

Queen's Medical Center
w queens.org

Straub Medical Center
w hawaiipacifichealth.org

PERSONAL SECURITY
Emergency Services
c 911

Safe Space Alliance
w safespacealliance.com

Travelers with Specific Requirements

Oʻahu extends a warm aloha to travelers with specific requirements. Due in large part to the Americans with Disabilities Act (ADA), most hotels, restaurants, and attractions provide wheelchair ramps, designated parking places, and accessible restrooms. Braille translations of elevator button panels and other important signs are commonplace.

Some of Oʻahu's main sights – such as Pearl Harbor and the Polynesian Cultural Center – provide American Sign Language interpreters upon advance request. Pearl Harbor also has closed captioning (CC) for their films and signs in braille. 'Iolani Palace has touch tours for visually impaired visitors.

Several tour companies offer specialist holiday packages: **Deaf Vacations** has tours with American Sign Language interpreters; **Tom Barefoot Tours** has wheelchair-accessible tours; and **New Directions Travel** offers holidays for neurodiverse travelers.

A number of beaches on the island offer access to all-terrain wheelchairs; see the **City and County of Honolulu** website for information. Meanwhile, **Wheelers of Hawaii**, offers wheelchair-accessible minivan rentals.

The Go Hawaii website (*see p113*) has useful information for travelers with specific requirements.

Time Zones

Unlike the US mainland, Hawaii does not subscribe to Daylight Savings Time. From October to April, it is two hours behind the US West Coast (10 hours behind GMT); from April to October it is three hours behind the West Coast (11 hours behind GMT).

Money

The currency in Oʻahu is the US dollar. VISA and MasterCard are universally accepted, except by the smallest stores and roadside stands. Most places accept Discover, Diners Club, and American Express, too. Contactless payments are becoming the norm in hotels, restaurants, stores, gas stations, and elsewhere in Oʻahu.

ATMs can be found in hotels, shopping centers, grocery stores, and outside most banks. In general, banks are open from 8:30am to 3 or 4pm Monday to Thursday, and from 8:30am to 6pm on Friday. Some branches are open on Saturdays. Bank of Hawaii and First Hawaiian Bank are Oʻahu's largest, with locations across the island.

Tipping is the norm in Hawaii. Around 15–20 per cent of the check is usual for waiting staff; around $1 per drink for bartenders. When traveling by taxi, 10–15 per cent of the fare is expected. Tip luggage handlers $1–2 a bag, housekeeping $2–5 a day, and valets $2–3.

Electrical Appliances

Standard US current is 110–120 volts. Non-US appliances will need a converter as well as a plug adapter with two flat pins.

Cell Phones and Wi-Fi

Before traveling, check with your cell-phone company about rates and travel packages. It is also possible to purchase an inexpensive cell phone from Walmart or a SIM card from AT&T, T-Mobile, Verizon or Hoku Wireless.

Wi-Fi is available at most condos and hotels, and it is often included in the rate. Many cafés, shopping centers, and restaurants also offer complimentary Wi-Fi.

Postal Services

Posting a letter in Oʻahu costs the same as on the US mainland, but mail sometimes takes longer to reach its destination. Hotels will often post mail for you, but otherwise there are post offices in every town. Opening hours are usually 8:30am to 4:30pm Monday to Friday.

Weather

Contrary to popular belief, Hawaii does have seasons. Rain is common from October to January, and summer is much warmer than winter. Big surf arrives on the north shores in winter; south swells delight surfers in summer. At sea level, day temperatures average high 70s to mid-80s° F (25–31° C) most of the year; night temperatures can drop to the 60s° F (15–19° C), and sometimes even to the 50s° F (10–13° C) in winter.

During heavy rains, Oʻahu's streams and rivers are susceptible to flash floods; it is best not to venture out on

hikes or unfamiliar drives during this time.

Opening Hours

Large shopping centers tend to open from 9am to 9pm Monday to Saturday; Sunday hours are usually shorter. Some supermarkets and convenience stores stay open 24 hours. Most retail stores are open on US holidays with the exception of Christmas Day, New Year's Day, and Hawaii state holidays, such as Prince Kūhiō Day (March 26).

The COVID-19 pandemic proved that situations can change suddenly. Always check before visiting attractions and hospitality venues for up-to-date hours and booking requirements.

Visitor Information

The **O'ahu Visitors Bureau** is the island's chapter of the Hawaii Visitors and Conventions Bureau (HVCB) and serves as the official source of information for visitors. The Go Hawaii website (see p113) also provides excellent information. The *Honolulu Magazine* and Hawaiian Airlines' in-flight magazine *Hana Hou!* are also great sources of information; access both online. For updated online coverage of local news and event listings, visit websites such as **Hawaii Reporter** and **MidWeek**.

Visitors keen to give back can volunteer with one of O'ahu's many local organizations – sessions range from native tree planting to beach cleaning. Check out the O'ahu Visitors Bureau website for opportunities via the Mālama Hawai'i program.

Local Customs

When visiting sacred sites and natural areas, don't take lava rocks, sand, or any other natural resource with you; don't even move rocks. Use marked paths, respect signage, and don't climb on any sites.

Trespassing is illegal on O'ahu. When exploring the island watch out for signs marked *kapu* (forbidden) as they often mean no trespassing.

Language

Hawaii is the only state in the US with two official languages – English and Hawaiian, or 'Ōlelo Hawai'i. Hawaiian is closely related to Tahitian, Samoan, and other Polynesian languages. Today, roughly 0.1 per cent of the population can speak it fluently, but this percentage is on the rise.

Taxes and Refunds

There is a 4 per cent sales tax on all goods and services; further county surcharges can add an extra 0.5 per cent. There are also hotel taxes (see below). Tax refunds are not offered to foreign visitors.

Accommodation

Hotel rooms in O'ahu are generally quite expensive, especially those at oceanfront resorts. You will also need to factor in tax (a total of 13.25 per cent for accommodations), possible resort fees (around $25 per day), and parking (around $20 per day). There are quite a lot of options, however, for budget visitors, including renting a room in a house or a condo, or staying at a B&B or local inn. Another alternative is camping under the stars via **Hawaii State Parks**.

Spring break, summer (especially June to August), and Christmas are the busiest times of year and prices rise accordingly. Book early to get the cheapest deals.

Places to Stay

Luxury Hotels

Aston Waikiki Sunset
MAP M7 ▪ 229 Paoakalani Ave ▪ 922 0511 ▪ www.aquaaston.com ▪ $$
Perfect for families, this high-rise condominium close to the beach features one- and two-bedroom suites with fully equipped kitchens. There's also a playground and a barbecue area.

Embassy Suites Waikiki Beach Walk
MAP K7 ▪ 201 Beachwalk St ▪ 921 2345 ▪ www.embassysuiteswaikiki.com ▪ $$
This all-suite hotel with impeccable amenities is ideal for families and groups. All guests enjoy spacious suites and a nightly poolside reception.

Hilton Hawaiian Village
MAP H6 ▪ 2005 Kālia Rd ▪ 949 4321 ▪ www.hiltonhawaiianvillage.com ▪ $$
Set on the widest stretch of popular Waikīkī Beach, this huge hotel has five towers, five pools, a lagoon, more than 80 shops, 18 lounges and restaurants, a spa, and tropical gardens.

Hyatt Regency Waikiki Beach Resort & Spa
MAP L7 ▪ 2424 Kalākaua Ave ▪ 923 1234 ▪ www.hyatt.com ▪ $$
An atrium with a cascading waterfall joins the two 40-story towers of this impressive Waikīkī resort. The seafood restaurant features open-air seating with ocean views.

Moana Surfrider, A Westin Resort & Spa
MAP K7 ▪ 2365 Kalākaua Ave ▪ 922 3111 ▪ www.marriott.com ▪ $$
Victorian elegance blends with modern comfort at this grand and historic beachfront hotel. It features six on-site dining options, a spa, gym, and an outdoor pool.

The Modern Honolulu
MAP G6 ▪ 1775 Ala Moana Blvd ▪ 943 5800 ▪ www.themodernhonolulu.com ▪ $$
In addition to stylish rooms, guests at this trendy resort enjoy a sunrise pool and a sunset beach. The hotel's pool bar is one of Honolulu's nightly hotspots.

Outrigger Reef Waikiki Beach Resort
MAP J7 ▪ 2169 Kālia Rd ▪ 923 3111 ▪ www.outriggerreef-onthebeach.com ▪ $$
Right on the beach near Fort DeRussy, this hotel's highlights include a pool, an oceanfront restaurant and bar, and nightly live music performances. It is also known for its Hawaiian-themed wedding vow renewal ceremonies.

Prince Waikiki
MAP G6 ▪ 100 Holomoana St ▪ 824 5155 ▪ www.princewaikiki.com ▪ $$
Each of the rooms at this marina-front hotel overlooks the picturesque Ala Wai Yacht Harbor. There are two award-winning restaurants: 100 Sails offers Hawaiian cuisine, while Katsumidori Sushi Tokyo has excellent Japanese fare. The hotel is very close to the Ala Moana Center, Waikīkī nightlife, and downtown Honolulu.

Turtle Bay Resort
MAP C1 ▪ 57–091 Kamehameha Hwy, Kahuku ▪ 293 6000 ▪ www.turtlebayresort.com ▪ $$$
On a stretch of oceanfront on the North Shore, this resort has rooms, beach cottages, and ocean villas. There are plenty of sports activities, and the on-site Nalu Spa offers a wide range of services.

Four Seasons Resort Oʻahu at Ko Olina
MAP B5 ▪ 92–1001 Olani St, Kapolei ▪ 679 0079 ▪ www.fourseasons.com ▪ $$$
With pools, tennis courts, golf, a cultural center, kids' activities, and top-notch restaurants, this is a plush five-star beach resort. Some suites have private gardens with plunge pools.

Halekulani
MAP J7 ▪ 2199 Kālia Rd ▪ 923 2311 ▪ www.halekulani.com ▪ $$$
This hotel on the beach has manicured tropical grounds, tasteful decor,

a spa, superb cuisine at La Mer (see p81), and its signature "orchid pool."

Marriott Ko Olina Beach Club

MAP B5 ■ 92-161 Waipahe Pl, Kapolei ■ 679 4700 ■ www.marriott.com ■ $$$
Stay in large, comfortable beachfront condos with high-end appliances, balconies, and several pools. The artificial lagoons of Ko Olina are ideal for kids to swim in.

The Ritz-Carlton Residences, Waikīkī Beach

MAP J5 ■ 383 Kalaimoku St ■ 922 8111 ■ www.ritzcarlton.com ■ $$$
Just a short walk from the beach, this establishment has ocean views from every spacious room, plus kitchenettes, a spa, and a 24-hour gym. The infinity pools are surrounded by private cabanas.

Royal Hawaiian Hotel

MAP K7 ■ 2259 Kalākaua Ave ■ 923 7311 ■ www.royal-hawaiian.com ■ $$$
Everything at the "Pink Palace of the Pacific," a Waikīkī landmark since 1927, is pink – from the stucco exterior to the towels. Its Royal Beach Tower is pricier, but many would say the Historic Wing has more charm.

Sheraton Waikiki

MAP K7 ■ 2255 Kalākaua Ave ■ 922 4422 ■ www.sheraton-waikiki.com ■ $$$
This sleek 1,700-room hotel towers over the beach at Waikīkī – most rooms have spectacular ocean views. You can admire Waikīkī's sparkling lights from the infinity pool bar and grill.

Mid-Range Hotels

Hotel La Croix

MAP J5 ■ 2070 Kalakaua Ave ■ 942 6006 ■ www.lacroixwaikiki.com ■ $
On the corner of two main streets at the north end of Waikīkī, this high-rise has a range of rooms to suit most budgets, and a saltwater infinity pool.

Park Shore

MAP M7 ■ 2586 Kalākaua Ave ■ 923 0411 ■ www.parkshorewaikiki.com ■ $
Located across from Kapiʻolani Park, at the Diamond Head end of Waikīkī, just steps from the beach, this hotel offers a premium location without premium prices. Rooms are comfortable, and there are three on-site restaurants to pick from.

Shoreline Hotel Waikīkī

MAP K6 ■ 342 Seaside Ave ■ 931 2444 ■ www.shorelinehotelwaikiki.com ■ $
This modern boutique hotel uses colorful, minimalist decor and natural motifs to evoke classic Hawaiian serenity. It is just steps from the beach and exclusive shopping options. The rooftop pool provides an optional escape from beach crowds.

The Laylow

MAP M6 ■ 2299 Kūhiō Ave ■ 922 6600 ■ www.laylowwaikiki.com ■ $$
A centrally located, pet-friendly hotel with mid-century modern rooms. Guests are treated to a lovely welcome basket of treats and a ukulele to play when they arrive.

Vive Hotel Waikīkī

MAP K6 ■ 2426 Kūhiō Ave ■ 687 2000 ■ www.vivehotelwaikiki.com ■ $
The Vive is located a few blocks from the beach. Although the modern rooms are on the smaller side, they are great value. The hotel offers complimentary Continental breakfast and beach gear to rent.

'Alohilani Resort

MAP L7 ■ 2490 Kalākaua Ave ■ 922 1233 ■ www.alohilaniresort.com ■ $$
In the middle of Waikīkī, this hotel is centered around a two-story-tall aquarium. Other features include a tennis court, pool and whirlpool, salon and spa, and lobby shops.

Aqua Oasis

MAP K6 ■ 320 Lewers St ■ 923 2300 ■ www.aquaaston.com ■ $
This boutique hotel off the main drag is a hidden treasure. One of the two towers has suites, while the other has regular rooms. Perks include a pool and sundeck, as well as free tickets to the Bishop Museum (see pp14–15) and the Honolulu Museum of Art (see pp24–25).

Diamond Head Beach Hotel & Residences

MAP E6 ■ 2947 Kalākaua Ave ■ 379 3718 ■ www.dhbhsuites.com ■ $$
The serene oceanfront setting at the base of Diamond Head, away from the bustle of Waikīkī, makes up for the simplicity of these condos just a short walk from Kalākaua Avenue's dining and shopping scenes.

Hilton Waikiki Beach
MAP M6 ▪ 2500 Kūhiō Ave ▪ 922 0811 ▪ www.hiltonwaikikibeach.com ▪ $$

A short walk to Kūhiō Beach, this hotel has an American restaurant, that's open 24 hours, and several bars, as well as a 10th-floor pool deck.

ʻIlima Hotel
MAP K6 ▪ 445 Nohonani St ▪ 923 1877 ▪ www.ilima.com ▪ $$

All the one-, two-, and three-bedroom suites and the studios are spacious, with en suite kitchens. Free parking is included in the rates, and there is free Wi-Fi too. A pool, exercise room, and sauna add to the experience.

Kaimana Beach Hotel
MAP M7 ▪ 2863 Kalākaua Ave ▪ 923 1555 ▪ www.kaimana.com ▪ $$

Rooms at this boutique hotel are small, but the Sans Souci Beach location, opposite Kapiʻolani Park, with easy access to the Honolulu Zoo and the Waikīkī Shell, more than makes up for it. The beachside Hau Tree Lanai restaurant offers an excellent brunch menu.

Lotus Honolulu at Diamond Head
MAP L7 ▪ 2885 Kalākaua Ave ▪ 922 1700 ▪ www.lotushonoluluhotel.com ▪ $$

This chic boutique hotel with a Zen vibe is just a short stroll from the beach. It offers ocean and mountains views, along with other facilities such as complimentary parking, wine tastings, and bike rentals.

Outrigger Waikiki Beach Resort
MAP K7 ▪ 2335 Kalākaua Ave ▪ 923 0711 ▪ www.outrigger.com ▪ $$

The 500 rooms at this oceanfront hotel, the jewel in the crown of the Outrigger chain, feature Polynesian decor. The popular beachfront Duke's Waikiki restaurant often hosts contemporary local entertainers.

Sheraton Princess Kaʻiulani
MAP L6 ▪ 120 Kaʻiulani Ave ▪ 922 5811 ▪ www.marriott.com ▪ $$

This hotel offers all the advantages of a Sheraton hotel without the ocean-front prices. Rooms have balconies, the pool bar is lovely, and there's a well-equipped gym.

Surfjack Hotel & Swim Club
MAP K5 ▪ 412 Lewers St ▪ 923 8882 ▪ www.surfjack.com ▪ $$

In a quiet area away from the beachfront, this boutique hotel has vintage decor and works of art by local artists. Enjoy poolside cocktails and a range of *pūpū* (appetizers) from the superb Mahina & Sun's restaurant *(see p81)*, or borrow free bikes for a ride around town.

Waikiki Beachcomber by Outrigger
MAP K6 ▪ 2300 Kalākaua Ave ▪ 922 4646 ▪ www.waikikibeachcomber.com ▪ $$

This beautifully decorated hotel is a stone's throw from the beach. All rooms include mini-fridges. Guests can also enjoy the outdoor pool and hot tub, and sunrise yoga classes.

Waikiki Shore
MAP J7 ▪ 2161 Kālia Rd ▪ 952 4500 ▪ www.castleresorts.com ▪ $$

Most of the one- and two-bed suites and studios at this oceanfront condo complex in Waikīkī feature breathtaking views, especially those on the upper floors. All units have a kitchen and laundry facilities.

Budget Hotels

Kailua Beach Properties
MAP F4 ▪ 204 S. Kalaheo Ave, Kailua ▪ 261 1653 ▪ www.patskailua.com ▪ $–$$$

Groups of friends or families who would like to experience Hawaii like locals would do well to consider staying at one of these fully furnished homes and cottages in beautiful residential areas of Kailua and Lanikai, on Oʻahu's windward side.

Ke ʻIki Beach Bungalows
MAP B1 ▪ 59–579 Keʻiki Rd, Haleʻiwa ▪ 638 8229 ▪ www.keikibeach.com ▪ $

These modern and comfortable beach cottages occupy their own stretch of sand between the surfing beaches of Waimea Bay and Banzai Pipeline. Run by a local resident, they offer family-style accommodation.

Pagoda Hotel
MAP B6 ▪ 1525 Rycroft St ▪ 941 6611 ▪ www.pagodahotel.com ▪ $

Popular with locals thanks to its proximity to the shops at Ala Moana, this hotel offers a variety

of rooms – standard, studios with kitchenettes, and suites. The private gardens and refreshing pool are a bonus.

Ramada Plaza by Wyndham Waikiki
MAP H6 ■ 1830 Ala Moana Blvd ■ 955 1111 ■ www.ramadaplaza waikiki.com ■ $
This 17-story high-rise hotel is at the gateway to Waikīkī and just two blocks from the beach. There's a pool with sundeck, and a fitness facility. There are no extra fees for facilities but there are parking charges.

Royal Grove Waikiki
MAP L6 ■ 151 Uluniu Ave ■ 923 7691 ■ www.royal grovewaikiki.com ■ $
Located in a convenient central area, this pink, family-run hotel oozes retro character. Guests can choose from a variety of rooms and don't have to pay a resort fee. There's a small pool and musical nights too.

White Sands Hotel
MAP K6 ■ 431 Nohonani St ■ 924 7263 ■ www. whitesandshotel.com ■ $
With simple rooms that have a fun, vintage vibe, this hotel is just two blocks from the beach. Rooms include mini-fridges, microwaves, and private balconies. The pool bar has swings and live music.

Inns and B&Bs

Diamond Head B&B
MAP E6 ■ 3240 Noela Dr, Honolulu ■ 923 3360 ■ www.diamondhead bnb.com ■ $
Situated at the base of Diamond Head, this namesake B&B is located

within walking distance of parks, beaches, and restaurants. The suites here are bright and roomy with private bathrooms, and the balconies open up to the lush garden in the back.

Kalani Hawaii
MAP B2 ■ 59–222 B. Kamahameha Hwy, Hale'iwa ■ 781 6415 ■ www.kalanihawaii.com ■ $
Located amid luscious green vegetation and expansive stretches of sand, Kalani Hawaii gives guests the opportunity to enjoy the island at its best. Choose from a range of rooms, houses, and studios in this North Shore resort.

Manoa Valley Inn
MAP C6 ■ 2001 Vancouver Dr ■ 926 0888 ■ www.manoa valleyinn.com ■ $$
This Victorian-style inn is located near the Univesity of Hawaii. Seven rooms and a single cottage provide guests with a quiet retreat from Honolulu's lights and action. Built in 1912, the Manoa Valley Inn is listed on the National Register of Historic Places.

Manu Mele Bed and Breakfast
MAP F4 ■ 153 Kailuana Pl, Kailua ■ 262 0016 ■ www.manumele.com ■ $
In a quiet suburban area near the beach, two comfortable suites with private entrances offer cooking facilities, air-conditioning, and complimentary Wi-Fi. The gardens and pool are an added bonus.

Papaya Paradise B&B
MAP F4 ■ 395 Auwinala Rd, Kailua ■ 261 0316 ■ www.windward-oahu. com ■ $
Friendly hosts offer two private units about half a mile (1 km) from the beach, in the residential section of Kailua. Great value for money, this place offers a backyard pool and shared kitchen.

Waimanalo Beach Cottages
MAP F5 ■ 41–10 Wailea St, Waimanalo ■ 427 9948 ■ www.waimanalobeach cottages.com ■ $$
Hunker down in one of the nine cottages at this quiet, beachfront resort. Accommodation includes full kitchen and free parking, and the cottages are also pet-friendly.

Rainbow Inn
MAP D4 ■ 98–1049 Mahola Pl, Aiea ■ 284 3995 ■ $
With its panoramic view of Pearl Harbor and large rooms, Rainbow Inn is great value for money. Its secluded location – as well as the ocean and mountains nearby and the friendly, helpful hosts – add to its charm.

Hawaii's Hidden Hideaway B&B
MAP F4 ■ 1369 Mokolea Dr, Kailua ■ 262 6560 ■ www.ahawaiibnb.com ■ $$
One of the island's top-rated B&Bs, this establishment is located right across the beach. It offers private entrances, bathtubs, and kitchen/dining areas, as well as complimentary beach items, a laundry, *lanai*, and excellent breakfasts.

For a key to hotel price categories see p116

General Index

Acknowledgments

This edition updated by

Contributor Lisa Voormeij
Senior Editor Alison McGill
Senior Art Editor Vinita Venugopal
Project Editors Dipika Dasgupta, Lucy Sara-Kelly
Project Art Editor Ankita Sharma
Editor Mark Silas
Picture Research Manager Taiyaba Khatoon
Picture Research Administrator Vagisha Pushp
Publishing Assistant Halima Mohammed
Jacket Designer Jordan Lambley
Senior Cartographer Subhashree Bharati
Cartography Manager Suresh Kumar
Senior DTP Designer Tanveer Zaidi
Senior Production Editor Jason Little
Senior Production Controller Samantha Cross
Deputy Managing Editor Beverly Smart
Managing Editors Shikha Kulkarni, Hollie Teague
Managing Art Editor Sarah Snelling
Senior Managing Art Editor Priyanka Thakur
Art Director Maxine Pedliham
Publishing Director Georgina Dee

DK would like to thank the following for their contribution to the previous editions:

The publisher would like to thank the following for their kind permission to reproduce their photographs:

Key: a-above; b-below/bottom; c-centre; f-far; l-left; r-right; t-top

123RF.com: fominayaphoto 46t; globalphoto 104–5; Joshua Rainey 87cr; sorincolac 4b; Svitlana Tereshchenko 58cl.

4Corners: Susanne Kremer 3tl, 66–7.

Aesthetic Hawaii Gallery: 100b

Alamy Stock Photo: James Au 63br; Tibor Bognar 22cl; Felix Choo 107br, Ian Dagnall 36bl; DanitaDelimont.com/ Charles Crust 62tl, / Michael DeFreitas 31bl; Design Pics Inc 77br, 97b / 770 Productions / Pacific Stock - RF 1; Douglas Peebles Photography 90c, 94tl; dpa picture alliance 102c; Robert Fried 32cla, 32br; Stephen Goodwin 78–9; Jeff Greenberg 40cl; H. Mark Weidman Photography 54br; Kelly Headrick 72cla, 95cla; Andre Jenny 103bl; Terry Kelly 82cl; Keith Levit 50-51; Ilene MacDonald 16clb; Angus McComiskey 98cla; Jon Mclean 45br; Leigh Anne Meeks 75cr; John De Mello 96cla; David L. Moore – Hawaii 14cl, 14–15, 38bc; Photo Resource Hawaii 15c, 15br, 19cr, 27cl, 57tr, 83t, 91tl,; PJF Military Collection 65cl; Rob Smith 39cl; SOTK2011 41c; David Wall 86br; Westend61 GmbH / Christian Vorhofer 88-89; Andrew Woodley 70cl.

AWL Images: Danita Delimont Stock 42tl; Michele Falzone 4cl; Nordic Photos 49tl.

Dreamstime.com: Adeliepenguin 16bl; Tomas Del Amo 6cla, 50tl; Aquamarine4 29tl, 63cl; Bennymarty 13bl, 50cr, 76c; Boreccy 30bl; James Crawford 19tl; Demerzel21 30–31; Eric Broder Van Dyke 4crb, 10clb, 73tl, 74bl, 77ca, 106tl; Eddygaleotti 11crb, 28–9; Edwardstewartii 41tl; Joel Ferrer 12cla; Yun Gao 103tr; Gilles Gaonach 43cl; Jose Gil 11br; Jerryway 46clb; Ritu Jethani 32-33ca; Klodien 13crb; Kungverylucky 59c; Ldionisio 62b; Rico Leffanta 23tl, 64bl; Viktoria Lelis 39tr; Chee-onn Leong 17br, Madrabothair 6br; 104clb; Mazikab 45c; Leigh Anne Meeks 43br; 48b, 91br, 105bl; Mkojot 52tr, 93cl, 99tl; MNStudio 4t, 53cl, 98–9; Shane Myers 2tr, 11cl, 34–5, 84cla; Glenn Nagel 17tl, 18–19, 64t; NatashaBreen 101cra; Mihaela Nica 4clb; Yooran Park 79bl; Photoblueice 33crb; Picturemakersllc 12–13; Marek Poplawski 36c; Ppy2010ha 58br; RightFramePhotoVideo 26–7; Shinnki 31tl; Daniel Shumny 29cr; Svetik48 61tr; Jayashri V 92t; Vacclav 10cla; Vasen 19br; Gerald Watanabe 27cb, 44bl, 45t, 84c; Ashley Werter 23br; Jeff Whyte 2tl, 8–9, 11cra, 16–17, 27tl, 68tr, 71cla, 78cl, 97cra.

Duke's Waikiki: 80t.

Getty Images: Rita Ariyoshi 59tl; Bill Bachmann 55cra; Ann Cecil 52b, 59br; Linda Ching 14br; David Inc 73crb; Design Pics / Ron Dahlquist 41br; Peter French 54t; Interim Archives 37cl; Lonely Planet Images 47bl; Cory Lum 65br; MyLoupe 12crb; Douglas Peebles 70b; Sri Maiava Rusden 61bl; Brandon Tabiolo 38t.

Honolulu Museum of Art: 11tr, 24br, 24–5, 25tl, 25c, 25br.

Hotel Halekulani: 56tl, 81bl.

Iolani Palace: The Friends of Iolani Palace 10br, 18cla, 18br.

Getty Images/iStock: BackyardProduction 3tr, 108–9; CampPhoto 49crb; compassandcamera 4cr; eyfoto 28cla; ilbusca 37br; KarenMassier 69tr; Kirkikis 20–21; LanaCanada 68cl, 92br; littlestocker 72b; nantela 82br; PB57photos 42b; tropicalpixsingapore 4cla; Kenneth Wiedemann 22cra.

Koko Head Cafe: 60t.

Rainbow Watersports: 53tr.

Robert Harding Picture Library: Michael

DeFreitas 84–5; North Light Images 7br;
Douglas Peebles 10bl; Greg Vaughn 40br.

Royal Hawaiian Hotel: 26cl.

Sansei Seafood Restaurant & Sushi Bar: 60bl.

Sunset Yoga Hawai'i: Charotte Davenport 57bl.

SuperStock: Prisma / Heeb Christian 85cl.

Cover

Front and spine: **Alamy Stock Photo:** Design
Pics Inc / 770 Productions / Pacific Stock - RF

Back: **123RF.com:** globalphoto crb;
Alamy Stock Photo: Cavan Images /
Aurora Photos / Sean Davey cla, Design
Pics Inc / 770 Productions / Pacific Stock -
RF b, Douglas Peebles Photography tl;
Dreamstime.com: Demerzel21 tr.

Pull Out Map Cover

Alamy Stock Photo: Design Pics Inc / 770
Productions / Pacific Stock - RF

All other images © Dorling Kindersley
For further information see:
www.dkimages.com

Penguin
Random
House

First Edition 2004

First published in Great Britain by
Dorling Kindersley Limited,
DK, One Embassy Gardens, 8 Viaduct
Gardens, London SW11 7BW, UK

The authorised representative in the EEA is
Dorling Kindersley Verlag GmbH. Arnulfstr.
124, 80636 Munich, Germany

Published in the United States by
DK Publishing, 1745 Broadway, 20th Floor,
New York, NY 10019, USA

Copyright © 2004, 2023 Dorling
Kindersley Limited
A Penguin Random House Company

23 24 25 26 10 9 8 7 6 5 4 3 2 1

A CIP catalog record is available
from the British Library.

A catalog record for this book is available
from the Library of Congress.

ISSN 1479 344X

ISBN 978-0-2416-2234-6

Printed and bound in Malaysia

www.dk.com

*As a guide to abbreviations in visitor information
blocks: **Adm** = admission charge; **D** = dinner.*

MIX
Paper | Supporting
responsible forestry
FSC™ C018179

This book was made with Forest
Stewardship Council™ certified
paper – one small step in DK's
commitment to a sustainable future.
**For more information go to
www.dk.com/our-green-pledge**

Phrase Book

Hawaiian began as an oral language and was put into written form by missionaries who arrived in the 1820s. The teaching and speaking of Hawaiian was banned from the early 1900s, and by the time the native cultural renaissance began in 1978 the melodious language was almost totally lost. Immersion programs are beginning to produce a new generation of Hawaiian speakers, however, and you will hear Hawaiian words sprinkled in conversation and in the islands' music, as well as seeing it written on some signs.

Summary of Pronunciation

The Hawaiian language has just 12 letters: the five vowels plus h, k, l, m, n, p, and w.

unstressed vowels:
a = as in "*a*bove"
e = as in "b*e*t"
i = as y in "cit*y*"
o = as in "s*o*le"
u = as in "f*u*ll"

stressed vowels:
ā = as in "f*a*r"
ē = as in "p*a*y"
ī = as in "s*ee*"
ō = as in "s*o*le"
ū = as in "m*oo*n"

consonants:
h = as in "*h*at"
k = as in "*k*ick"
l = as in "*l*aw"
m = as in "*m*ow"
n = as in "*n*ow"
p = as in "*p*in"
w = as in "*w*in" or "*v*ine"

The 'okina (glottal stop) is found at the beginning of some words beginning with vowels or between vowels. It is pronounced like the sound between the syllables in the English "uh-oh."

ali'i = ahlee-ee
liliko'i = leeleekoh-ee
'ohana = oh-hahnah

The kahakō (macron) is a mark found only above vowels, indicating vowels should be stressed.

kāne = kah-nay
kōkua = koh-koo-ah
pūpū = poo-poo

Everyday Words

aloha	ah-loh-ha	hello; goodbye; love
hale	ha-leh	house
hula	who-la	Hawaiian dance
kāhiko	kaa-hee-koh	old, traditional
kapa	kah-pah	bark cloth
keiki	kay-kee	child
kōkua	koh-koo-ah	help
lānai	luh-nigh	porch; balcony
lei	layh	garland
lua	looah	bathroom
mahalo	muh-ha-low	thank you
'ono	oh-noh	delicious
ko'olau	koh-oh-lowh	windward side

Geographical and Nature Terms

'a'ā	ah-*aah*	rough, jagged lava
kai	kaee	ocean
koholā	koh-hoh-*laah*	humpback whale
mauna	mau-nah	mountain
pāhoehoe	pah-hoy-hoy	smooth lava
pali	pah-lee	cliff
pu'u	poo-oo	hill
wai	w(v)hy	fresh water

Historical Terms

ali'i	ahlee-ee	chief; royalty
heiau	hey-yow	ancient temple
kahuna	kah-hoo-nah	priest; expert
kapu	kah-poo	taboo
kupuna	koo-poo-nah	elders; ancestors
luakini	looh-ah-kee-nee	human sacrifice temple
mana	mah-nah	supernatural power
mele	meh-leh	song
oli	oh-leeh	chant

Food Words

'ahi	ah-hee	yellowfin tuna
aku	ah-koo	skipjack; bonito
a'u	ah-oo	swordfish; marlin
haupia	how-peeah	coconut pudding
kalo	kah-loh	taro
kālua	kah-*looah*	food baked slowly in an underground oven
laulau	lau-lau	steamed filled ti-leaf packages
liliko'i	lee-lee-koh-ee	passion fruit
limu	lee-moo	seaweed
lomi-lomi salmon	low-me low-me	raw salmon with onion and tomato
lū'au	*loo*-ow	Hawaiian feast
mahimahi	muh-hee-muh-hee	dorado; dolphin fish
poi	poy	pounded taro
pūpū	*poo-poo*	appetizer
uku	oo-koo	gray snapper
ulua	oo-*looah*	jackfish

Pidgin

Hawaii's unofficial conglomerate language is commonly heard on the street and in backyards throughout Hawaii. You may hear:

brah	brother, pal
broke da mout'	great food
fo' real	really
fo' what	why
grinds	food; also to grind
howzit?	how's everything?
kay den	okay then
laydahs	later; goodbye
no can	cannot
no mo' nahting	nothing
shoots!	yeah!
stink eye	dirty look
talk story	chat; gossip